MONTANA
FOLKS

MONTANA
FOLKS

Durrae and John Johanek

Photographs by Kurt Keller

TWODOT®

GUILFORD, CONNECTICUT
HELENA, MONTANA

AN IMPRINT OF THE GLOBE PEQUOT PRESS

A · T W O D O T® · B O O K

Text design by Clare Cunningham

Library of Congress Cataloging-in-Publication Data is available.

ISBN 0-7627-2546-X

Manufactured in China
First Edition/First Printing

To Brett Favre, Michael Jordan, and Dan Gremmer

—John and Durrae Johanek

✦

For my grandfather, Gene Baldensperger, with thanks for his

knowledge, encouragement, and inspiration

—Kurt Keller

CONTENTS

PREFACE

This is our Honda CRV's second book. Not that we want to give the manufacturer a plug, but it's seen more of Montana than most pickups and never once complained. Our first book, *Montana Behind the Scenes,* covered lesser-known places. Besides being a great excuse to travel Big Sky Country, we wanted people to know that there was more to Montana than just Yellowstone and Glacier National Parks. In *Montana Folks* we focus on the backbone of the state—its people—and chip away at the stereotype that we're just a bunch of beef-eating cowboys (not that there's anything wrong with that—some of our best friends are cowboys who eat beef). The reality is that Montana encompasses a wide range of occupations and interests, and it would have taken 900,000 chapters, one for each Montanan, to cover them all.

There are plenty of books on pioneers and homesteaders and "older than dirt" folks who have stories to tell, but as important as that is to our history, it's not what we were looking for. We wanted the people we see every day—at the market, in the post office, pumping gas—our neighbors and fellow statesmen. After hundreds of hours of contacting newspapers and chambers of commerce and stopping strangers on the street, we hit the road to see firsthand the faces behind the saddle maker, cherry grower, mortician, bullfighter, and botanist,

as well as a few stereotypes, all unique to Montana or uniquely Montanan.

Although most people we contacted for leads were wonderful, it wasn't all gravy: Many didn't return calls and a few gave us the bum's rush, but we were dogged. Scheduling interviews was another unexpected hassle—it turns out not everyone was in tune to our schedule, and a few backed out at the last minute. Again we persisted and are happy to note no doors were slammed on us.

But the toughest part was keeping each chapter to one thousand words; so many could have filled an entire book. Another dilemma was who would be the first chapter, and we picked Janet Zieg for two reasons. First, everything we do in Montana is dictated by the weather, and that's her specialty. Second, with a last name like Zieg, we figured she seldom gets listed first. And of course someone had to go last, and who better to lay the book to rest than Bill Bell, a mortician. As for the others, what you see here is what you get when you pull names out of a hat, a cowboy hat no less.

While adding 12,000 miles to our car's odometer, we saw lots of the state, sometimes at ridiculous speeds to make an interview on time. And true to Montana's reputation, the weather wasn't always cooperative: We were hailed, rained, and snowed on; baked in Broadus; frozen along the Hi-line; and nearly blown into the Missouri

Breaks. Visibility was so bad from forest fires at times that we actually saw meadowlarks walk across the road. We've gotten just a bit smarter about traveling the back roads since our first book and didn't get sucked in, literally, by gumbo (that's Montana mud). Although we took full advantage of Montana's speed limit (we were never pulled over for driving too slow), we often stopped to marvel at a sunset, watch an eagle descend on a ground squirrel, or ooh and aah over formations in the badlands.

All along the way we were entertained with special performances: Sandy and Owen James jammed on the piano and fiddle, Sam Hofer's daughters sang angelic a cappella, Paul Zarzyski waxed poetic, and Wayne Phillips yodeled. We even tipped a few brews with Santa himself, who in shorts and Hawaiian print shirt didn't fool anyone. We were given grand tours of the museum at Fort Benton, Missoula's carousel, and Our Lady of the Rockies, and fiddled around in Rosebud with Jack Schwend.

Without exception everyone in the book emphasized how influential other people—parents, friends, siblings—were in their lives. And some, like Bob O'Bill, Lady of the Rockies; Jerry Diettert, Carousel for Missoula; and Charles Patten of the Broadus Cattle Drive, wanted to be sure we mentioned that they're just one of many volunteers involved with each of their pursuits.

Southern hospitality can't hold a candle to the way we were welcomed. Sometimes we stayed longer than we planned, but our hosts were always gracious and usually waited until we left before they started eating dinner. In spite of our persistence, we've made new friends along the way. We hope you enjoy reading about these folks as much as we enjoyed meeting them.

—John and Durrae Johanek

PHOTOGRAPHER'S NOTE

Sitting on the porch of the isolated ranch house staring into the misty rain, I contemplate the return trip over the gumbo road that I had traversed in the sun some two hours before. Waiting for a sign of the branding party somewhere out on this massive southeastern Montana ranch, I wonder if I'll make my next appointment. It's at least two-and-a-half hours to Glendive and I'm to be there in three hours. An hour later I give in and admit I will have to reschedule.

The relaxing sound of nothing but the rain brings a smile to my face as I consider the possibility of spending the night on the ranch while all belongings except my photography gear spend the night in my Miles City hotel room. I think back to when I was first approached about this project and I couldn't believe my good fortune. Let me get this right? You want me to drive all over the beautiful Montana landscape to meet and photograph interesting people. More than 10,000 miles and 2,500 exposures later, I would start all over again tomorrow.

The goal for me on the project was not just to show what these people look like, but what these people are like. In all but two cases I worked independently from John and Durrae. I refrained from reading any chapters that they might have already written before I met and photographed the subject. This practice would help me form independent ideas through my own interaction with these people. In order to get more insight into how they lived and other interests in their lives, I tried to meet all the folks at their home or place of business. I was amazed at how gracious everyone was, welcoming me into their home or business and in most cases both! Although our subjects did know I was coming to photograph them, I made no suggestions on clothing or outfit choices. I spent anywhere from a half hour to nearly a whole day with the subjects. In most cases very little time was spent making photographs. Most of our time was spent exchanging life experiences and taking tours of pertinent locations in their lives. I went into each situation as an adventure. I knew very little about location and had spoken on the phone with these people only a few times. I had no preconceived idea of what I wanted to do and just let the settings and personality reveal themselves. These photos were not "posed." The most direction I would give would be, "Why don't you sit over there." In most cases we were in a conversation and I would say, "Let's do a photo here," and as we talked I would make photographs.

As far as equipment goes, I used everything from 35mm to 4x5 cameras on this project. My RB67 medium-format camera was the most used piece of equipment during the project. I am old school in my equipment selection; I don't even own an automatic-focus camera, let alone a digital camera. All images were captured on black-and-white films. I tried to use available light whenever I could. In many situations this meant long exposures of a quarter to a half a second. In a few situations I was forced to use studio lights.

The moan of a straining engine breaks the silence and brings me back to the present. It's stopped raining for the moment and I can see a pickup truck summit a distant hill. Moments later a 1960s model flatbed pulls up to the porch and the door opens. I am about to start another adventure through *Montana Folks.*

—*Kurt Keller*

———◆———

As this book was being finalized, we received the news that Blanche Harding (page 29) and Esther Dean (page 161) had passed away. We feel fortunate to have met them and are grateful that we can share that experience with you here in our book.

ACKNOWLEDGMENTS

Special thanks to Kurt Keller, master of photography and all-around nice guy. Thanks, too, to editor Megan Hiller, who guided us and had incredible patience with all our questions, but we do wonder why she moved to Maine halfway through the book. And a hearty thank you to Scott McMillion, who, even though he didn't make the book with his killer chili, got us pointed in the right direction.

And to all the people listed here, if it weren't for your help, *Montana Folks* would still be just an idea: Terry Anderson, Jan Bauer, Bruce Becker, Sheryl Berger, Mary Birac, Lois Blasberg, Mary Cates, Theresa Cox, Gordon Dean, Pete Dean, Rick Dittmann, Marge Dobeck, Patty Eisle, Jillian and Parker Fink, John Foster, Bob Gough, Ray Grant, Beau Heath, Nancy Hedrick, Debbie Herrington, Lora Heyen, Kathy Kellogg, Mary Kenison, Rory Kremer, Stan Krenz, Ed Kurdy, Lynn Laurandeau, Herman Linder, David Merrill, Tim Miles, Lou Moro, Carol O'Dell, Leon Old Elk–Stewart, Jeanne Portwine, Fran Rogers, Pete and Kandy Rose, Bruce Selyem, Kenny Shields, Dan Sowle, Ray Trumpower, Twila Talcott, Sara Toubman, Dave Walter, JoDee Watson, Candace White, Matt Wilhelm, Ryan Yeager, Tony Zitterkopf.

—*John and Durrae Johanek*

Special thanks to my family for their support and understanding as they dealt with an absentee husband and father for many extended weekends throughout the project.

Sincere thanks to all the "Montana folks" and their families for their hospitality and kindness as they welcomed me into their homes and places of business. Once again I have been shown why Montana is such a unique and truly special place.

Special thanks to Megan Hiller and Erin Turner for bringing me into the project and pushing the book forward.

Last but not least, thanks to John and Durrae Johanek for welcoming me into their idea and keeping me laughing the whole time.

—*Kurt Keller*

Her great-grandfather started doing it back in 1910. When he died, her grandmother took over. Then her mother did it for twenty-eight years. Now Janet Zieg does it every day. For nearly a century they've been watching the skies and recording the weather. Loved, hated, misunderstood—wherever locals gather for morning coffee, it's a hot topic even on the coldest day. The talk eventually turns from the weather outside to "I remember when . . ." stories. And Janet "remembers when" better than anybody around because for dozens of years she's written it all down. Off the top of her head she can tell you that on her ranch near White Sulphur Springs, the record high temperature is ninety-seven degrees. The coldest day was February 4, 1989, when her thermometer bottomed out at minus forty-four, and the average annual snowfall is 160 inches.

Since 1965 Janet's been one of the National Weather Service (NWS) Cooperative

WEATHER OBSERVER

JANET ZIEG, WHITE SULPHUR SPRINGS

Weather Observers, a group of volunteers scattered throughout the country who collect weather data, a concept begun more than two hundred years ago by Thomas Jefferson. With a goal of establishing an observation site every 25 miles, the network now has more than eleven thousand observers nationwide—about three hundred in Montana alone.

The data have far-reaching effects. They're used in everything from architectural design and aviation to commerce and even litigation—the observations are critical to formulating NWS weather warnings. But in Montana the information has a far more important role. Over time patterns give a more accurate picture and help predict drought, winds, and storms. "We're in a drought cycle now," she says. "We can't predict when it will end but know it won't be soon."

During her childhood Janet's father worked for the Forest Service near Martinsdale. She got her introduction to weather tracking one fire season when a ranger stopped by the ranch to see if she'd be interested in monitoring the service's basic equipment as well as wind speed and humidity. She's not sure if that's what piqued her interest or if it came from watching her mother compile daily weather reports. Maybe it was the colorful silk weather balloons she found while horseback riding. "The balloons had an instrument box attached to them with instructions to return them," Janet recalls. "But because the weather service was interested only in the data, we kept the silk and used it to make blouses." When the NWS approached Janet to volunteer, "I was thrilled to death, and my mother encouraged me to do it," she says. Her weather instruments were packed up and taken along to the new Zieg ranch a few miles away in the Little Belt Mountains, much to the delight of the weather service, which wanted to keep an observer in the area.

Being a weather observer suits the ranching lifestyle. "We're home most of the time, and if we go, it's not too far or for too long." She takes her daily readings at the same time every evening, arranging for someone to read them if she's gone for an extended period. In addition to recording daily highs and lows and precipitation amounts, she makes note of any unusual conditions. Once a month she sends her report to the main office in Great Falls. At one time at her former ranch, she also collected data on water levels in the nearby Smith River. Twice a day she lowered a weighted rope, logged in the depth, and called that information in, too. Now those readings are done electronically.

Not every observer has the same equipment. "I have the basics," she says. "Some sites—ranger stations, for example—have much more sophisticated instruments than I do." The standard gauges that were once housed in small louvered towers in backyards across the country have given way to high-tech instruments that deliver digital readouts into her home. Snowfall is collected and melted to determine moisture content, but when it comes to snow depth, she still relies on the low-tech system—a stick pounded into the yard with measurements painted in calibrations large enough to see from her office window.

She never took any meteorological classes, although she's looking into correspondence courses, and she can't name all the cloud formations, "but I can look out the window and tell you which ones are bringing in a front." Each night she listens to the Great Falls and Helena weather stations to compare her data with theirs. "They don't give as many highs and lows as they used to," she laments, so Janet has turned to reality TV—getting hooked on the Weather Channel.

Recent federal budget cuts mean funding is a problem, and some home observation stations are being eliminated, but it's certainly not because of *her* salary—once every three months she receives a check for $12.51. However, some things are priceless. In 2000 she was singled out as one of twenty-five weather observers nationally to receive the prestigious National Oceanic and Atmospheric Administration John Campanius Holm Award—

"for outstanding accomplishment and diligence in the field of meteorological observation."

Montanans tend to be a hardy bunch, especially when it comes to weather. Old-timers refer to minus seventy degrees as "a bit nippy," and windchill isn't even part of their vocabulary. "Like it or not, it governs us," Janet says. Whatever the conditions, it has a big impact on how we live. Low snowpack and we're short of stock and irrigation water, a freak spring snowstorm and livestock suffers, too hot and fly fishing is banned and we're looking at a bad fire season. Every aspect of our economy is affected by the weather.

By 6:00 P.M. Janet has recorded her last bit of data and is ready to turn on the tube to compare her notes with the weather report. She takes one last look out the window at the snow stick before closing her notebook and punching the remote's "on" button. The phone rings. It's her neighbor asking year-to-date precipitation numbers. Janet goes back to her notebook. Her day's not finished yet. ✦

The grandstand is packed with rodeo fans. They've enjoyed everything from goat roping to barrel racing but know the best is coming up, and even a greenhorn spectator can sense the excitement. The announcer bellows the next event and the crowd goes nuts—this is what they've been waiting for. On cue a really unhappy-looking bull with a cowboy on its back charges out of the gate, throws the rider, then heads for the guy with red suspenders and clown face—the bullfighter—who springs into action to distract the stomping animal from the now vulnerable cowboy. Then with the bull's breath warming the back of his neck, the clown jumps the fence not a horntip too soon. The fans are ecstatic, but for bullfighter Loyd Ketchum it's a typical day.

The announcer lets you know the bull rider is the number one guy, but it's the bullfighter who saves number one's butt. This is not to confuse the fighter with the rodeo clown, who is usually stationed in a barrel and whose antics are mostly to entertain the audience.

It takes a special person to get into the ring with the sole intent of protecting the rider, and Loyd has saved numerous lives. His colorful bright suspenders, clown makeup, and patchwork endorsements are strictly for the crowd—the bull sees only black and white. His only physical protection—a pair of shin guards—is against the rider's spurs; against the bull, it's pure wit and athleticism.

If you were looking for a poster boy for bullfighting, it wouldn't be Loyd. With an average physique, weighing in at 150 pounds, he's no body builder, but by eating right and with daily exercise, he's lean and in top shape. Equally striking is his personality—quiet, calm, and modest—not what you'd imagine in someone who enjoys facing a ton of angry meat.

BULLFIGHTER

LOYD KETCHUM, MILES CITY

It's not surprising that Loyd developed an interest in the rodeo, having grown up on a ranch in the heart of Montana's cowboy country near Miles City. He didn't start life by looking at the business end of a big cow while surrounded by adoring fans. While attending college on a rodeo scholarship, he worked as a bull rider but decided he would rather help save the rider, and turned instead to bullfighting. That was back in 1984. Setting aside his degree in mechanics, he now spends two hundred days a year on the road performing in nearly thirty shows from Canada to South America.

To fill in between gigs, Loyd runs a small ranch where he breeds rodeo bulls. But although a top-quality animal sells for about $30,000, he notes that it's far from being a profit-making operation and more a labor of love. "Rodeo bulls have rap sheets, and we get to know them," he says, "and I know some better than others—I've even faced a few of my own in competition."

Loyd isn't the only bullfighter in the country, but he's one of the best and is highly respected by his peers (check out his Web site at www.loydketchum.com, which lists his accomplishments), and like any celebrity he has his own fan club. According to Loyd, "You need to be a good athlete, with superior reflexes and quick on your feet. Most important, you need to be able to read the bull, not something that comes easily for city kids." Today's bulls have the points of their horns cut off. Still, it's a dangerous—some might say insane—sport, but Loyd assures you that there are more dairy farmers killed by Holstein bulls.

Even the best athlete gets sidelined. For Loyd it was in Kansas that a bull gored him in the hip, requiring surgery, but thirty days later, held together with pins, wires, and screws he was back in the ring. It's Las Vegas, however, that brings to mind his worst rodeo moment. His demeanor changes when he talks about the kid who was killed after being stepped on. "There was nothing I could do about it," he says sadly. But Vegas also gave Loyd some of his best memories, particularly when he was crowned Wrangler World Champion

Bullfighter in 1991. And he was invited to protect the cowboy riders there five times, which is more prestigious than the competition itself.

The National Finals Rodeo is *the* event to shoot for, and Loyd is doing his part to help put others in front of its rampant bulls; he conducts schools for kids who want to learn his craft. But for those who are merely curious, Loyd talks to school groups when he's not busy staring down a bull—on any rodeo morning he can wow up to two hundred kids with his stories. No wonder his fan club is growing.

How long can Loyd take a bovine pounding and stay fit, and how long will it be before he realizes that an out-of-control bull can do serious bodily harm? "As long as I can keep people safe, I'll do it," he says. "I still don't know what I want to do when I grow up." ◆

Fly fishing is one of Montana's most popular drawing cards, and to the avid fly fisher—is there any other kind?—George Grant represents all that is good about the sport. There would be no fly fishing without flies, and George created some of the best.

He developed an interest in fly fishing in his early twenties. Whether it was family influence or location to the best trout streams in the world, George found first his hobby, then his vocation in stalking trout. Unlike the rest of his family, who fished with bait, he used a bamboo rod and hand-tied flies to cast in his favorite haunt, the Big Hole River.

Born in Butte in 1906 but lacking the physique to work in the local mines, he found his calling as a personal secretary and later stenographer in the railroad industry. Even in the heart of the Great Depression, George lived every die-hard fly fisher's dream—he passed up opportunities to advance in the business world, opting instead to live in a cabin on the Big Hole River and fish every day from spring through fall for the next four years. The river became George's first love.

George was an inquisitive soul, and he began taking apart the flies created by other tiers. Although they disintegrated as soon as he untied them, it wasn't long before he successfully dismantled one. The more he fished, the more he refined his skills in tying flies of his own design. In 1937 George hired an attorney to ensure that his flies were indeed unique.

During World War II, at the "old" age of thirty-six, he reported for duty but was turned down because of his poor eyesight, which was ironic because he was tying up to five thousand flies each year commercially, an occupation certainly not meant for the weak sighted. A few months later the army decided George wasn't such a bad candidate after all and drafted him because of

FLYTIER

GEORGE GRANT, BUTTE

his business experience. They quickly realized what they had, promoting him from buck private to staff sergeant in only six months. Trout kept him in Butte after the war, but the area's growing development troubled him.

Friends asked him to manage an outdoor supply store in West Yellowstone. George says, "With nothing else to do and living near the Madison, it was easy to get hooked." And he fished—"every minute I could." While working at sporting goods shops, including for a while his own, he and his wife, Annabell, whom he married in 1947, managed to eke out a living doing what he loved. Although Annabell was not interested in fishing when they met, George taught her to fish, and "she got real good at it," he says.

In 1951 he asked *Field and Stream* about writing an article but was rejected, which discouraged him from writing for nearly two decades. Little did anyone know that years later he'd not only become published but also known worldwide, so well known that a Japanese man made a special trip to Montana so George could autograph his copy of *The Art of Weaving Hair Hackles for Trout Flies.*

George's love of the Big Hole quickly grew into a major concern for the preservation of this special land. While others marveled at the progress growing out of mining, ranching, and tourism, George fought to deter environmental degradation such as clear-cutting, dam construction, and crop irrigation, often making headway where others had faltered. His stand on land loss and pollution often got him into deep trouble with ranchers. But the Big Hole River Foundation, which he was instrumental in establishing, provided funds for stream restoration, education, and even an irrigation system or two for local ranchers.

You can't tie flies without knowing fish, and George knows them well. His techniques for landing trophy trout are based on his acute understanding of fish habits and habitat.

George's signature hair hackle, the Black Creeper, imitates the salmon fly larva, which to a trout is a Big Mac on a string.

For the fly-fishing-challenged, a hackle represents the legs of a fly; it comes in two types, wet and dry, the dry being stiffer to float on the surface and the wet to sink. George is one of the few people to tie hair hackles, a tedious job that takes twenty minutes to half an hour versus three to four minutes for a standard fly.

Different flies for different fish, streams, and seasons—a conversation with George will yield valuable information on these topics. He'll tell you nymphs are best in winter: "You would catch trout with their snouts flattened from trying to get at nymphs under rocks." He'll also let you in on which streams are best: "Western Montana has the best trout streams in the world. The Madison is wider and faster and good in winter; the Yellowstone is good but can be too big. The Big Hole is good anytime. It's the model you'd use if you were going to build a trout stream."

Although trout are duped by a well-crafted fly, it takes a fisher to fully appreciate these miniature works of art. The materials range from monofilament to skunk tail, badger, elk, and deer hair, all of which can be found in George's flies. About eighty fly plates and flies from his personal collection have found a permanent home at the Butte Chamber of Commerce, and another thirty-five are on display at the International Flyfishing Federation museum in Livingston.

As a champion for nature in general and trout streams in particular, George Grant has earned his place among fly fishing's pioneers. Several of his many accomplishments stand out: He was the major proponent of catch and release; the Big Hole River and its unique grayling population exist today through his efforts; and among others, he's won the Chevron Oil environmental award and the Buszek award, which is given to a person in the field who has shared his knowledge and taught others. And he has tied some mighty pretty flies. ◆

Lots of people think the U.S. government is a Mickey Mouse operation, but Wayne Williams insists he owes his government career to Walt Disney himself. The Missoula-based smokejumper recalls, "When I was a kid growing up in California I saw the movie *A Fire Called Jeremiah* and knew then that jumping from an airplane into forest fires was what I wanted to do." Ironically that Disney-produced movie was filmed in Missoula in 1960.

While in high school he started looking into smokejumping schools and found that California had established a program called the Ecology Corps, in which conscientious objectors during the Vietnam War could do alternative service fighting forest fires. As the war wound down, the ranks were filled in with draft dodgers, returning veterans, and people like Wayne. Ecology Centers were set up in old inmate camps and run under the jurisdiction of the California Division of

SMOKEJUMPER

WAYNE WILLIAMS, MISSOULA

Forestry. Wayne enrolled so he could get experience working on wildfires. "In spite of our diverse and contrasting backgrounds, we all got along incredibly well. I think it's because even though we all had different convictions, we felt strongly about them and stuck to them," he says.

The $100 a month plus room and board was barely enough to get by, but he stuck it out for fourteen months until he took a job at the Eldorado National Forest near Lake Tahoe. It was during his two fire seasons there that he tried skydiving, just for the fun of it (if you call leaping from a plane at 5,000 feet fun)—that did it; he was hooked. The jump cost a wallet-busting $35, but he and his buddies wanted to see if they had what it took. "I had a really hard landing [unusual, he later found out] and wondered how long my body would hold up," he recalls—but it didn't stop him from taking the next step. He applied to several smokejumping schools, and when he heard from the one in Missoula, he stopped looking and packed his bags. But then he had to get there, and upstart firefighters are on a shoestring budget, so he hopped a freight train to his uncle's place in Whitefish—a short jump to Missoula.

That was in the mid-1970s. Since then his career has been punctuated with highlights of Montana's wildfire history. The worst fire disaster was the 1949 Mann Gulch fire north of Helena, where thirteen firefighters died when they were overtaken by flames. That was before Wayne's time, but since then Montana has had worse fire seasons but never as bad a loss of life, partly because of what was learned at Mann Gulch. Wayne's—and the state's—worst season was in 2000, and not surprisingly he was involved with the Yellowstone fire in 1988. "Who wasn't?" he says. "If you were alive and had a tool in your hand, you were there."

He doesn't fight fires only in Montana. New Mexico's fire season starts before ours, and he works out of a subbase there until mid-July,

when Montana's season begins to heat up. "I've fought fires everywhere except the New England states, where they have no consistent fire season," he says. But not all of his time is spent beating back flames.

At the Missoula Smokejumper Center the crew is constantly looking for ways to improve what they do and how they do it, including manufacturing and building most of their own gear. You'll find them hunched over sewing machines making packs and jumpsuits and repairing parachutes. They're always busy working up prototypes.

Technology has helped over the years, but it still comes down to the basics. "Firefighting used to be one-dimensional—you'd pretty much put the fire out and go home," says Wayne. "Now it's more complicated; people are living in the woods." Crews employ "burning out" and backfires to remove the fuel source (dried downfall) before a fire gets to it and perform prescribed burns to remove underbrush before the fire season starts, which can make a difference in how quickly a fire can be controlled or contained. Wayne clarifies the jargon: "If a fire is 100 percent contained, it means the crew has it completely surrounded, but it can still flare up and jump the fire line. When it's controlled, the crew has it comfortably managed and it poses little further danger."

The 450 or so smokejumpers in the United States (about thirty are women) are considered a national resource. Many who joined during the Vietnam era as Wayne did are turning fifty and eligible for retirement, thus creating a huge deficit of experienced firefighters. Rookies are trained for six weeks and weeded out if they don't perform. Even veterans like Wayne are required to take a two-week refresher course each year.

Smokejumpers and hot shots (specialized ground crew) are considered the elite because they have the most training and often go into a fire first, usually right into the heart of it. Wayne doesn't leap into every fire but gets in about ten jumps a year—half are practice. Although ground crew casualties can be high, deaths from smokejumping are minimal—just four out of about 300,000 jumps. He notes, "One was equipment failure; the other three were due to jumper error."

Smokejumping isn't as risky as you might think; it doesn't even rank in the top ten most dangerous professions. It has a good safety record because of the type of people it attracts and hires. "Only two wildfires are responsible for all of the smokejumper fatalities. The number one thing you need to be a jumper is common sense. It's not all brawn," Wayne says. But, according to one regional forester back in the 1930s when the concept was in its infancy, "All parachute jumpers are more or less crazy—just a little bit unbalanced, otherwise they wouldn't be engaged in such a hazardous undertaking." Wayne would disagree: "We're pretty rational people. Most folks are wrong: We're not the last cowboys." ◆

"Did you know that some of Montana's bridges were ordered from a catalog?" It's true, says Jon Axline. In fact, there's very little about our state's roadside history that he doesn't know. Not bad for a guy who actually hated local history as a kid. He went to Montana State University with every intention of studying ancient Greece and Rome but one day sat down with a copy of A. B. Guthrie's *Big Sky*, and the rest truly is history.

He half jokingly refers to his first job as assistant curator at the Old Prison Museum in Deer Lodge as "my time in prison," and he didn't mind leaving when the Museum of the Rockies hired him to organize the state history collection. When funds shrank and Jon's position was axed, he landed in Helena at the Department of Transportation. They wanted him to update the Roadside Information Sign project and write a history on the state's bridges. Jon didn't have much

ROADSIDE HISTORIAN

JON AXLINE, HELENA

knowledge about either but became passionate about both.

You've seen his work—large signs adjacent to pullouts throughout the state. The project, begun in 1935 by Bob Fletcher, was revamped in 1986, but under protest. Jon notes, "Devotees said, Sure, go ahead and install new signs and repair the existing ones but don't change the originals." The familiar redwood planks mounted between upright timbers remain as much a part of the landscape as cattle guards and barbwire.

Sign junkies can't pass one by. Numbering 170 sites and growing, they're roadside *Cliffs Notes* for the motorized historian. When the project began, Fletcher intentionally let color and folklore take a front seat to fact. Jon's goal is to keep people reading but smooth over the inaccuracies and make the content politically correct: "I used to get angry letters about the wording." There aren't any statistics on how many people actually stop to read the signs, but Jon does see them do it. "I'm often tempted to ask them what they think," he says.

Sometimes people call him about errors on a sign or want one in their area for something they think warrants special mention. Jon felt that Pompeys Pillar needed a marker because of the story about the Sioux warriors hiding behind the pillar and harassing Custer's men while they bathed in the river. "I love the image it conjures," he laughs. He likes hearing the Native American side of things and always gets the tribe's approval for signage at any sacred spot. Jon never erects a sign at an archaeological site: "I don't want to call attention to it."

The next time you see a road being built, a highway rerouted, or a bridge being replaced, you can bet that Jon has already been there. He thoroughly researches the history of the area surrounding every such project to determine what, if any, historical significance might need to be noted, preserved, or protected.

When road maintenance crews see damaged signs that need replacing, Jon jumps into action again. But as with just about any government job, "the biggest headache is the money. If we do it as part of a highway project, it's factored into the price, but if we want to put a sign at a new historical site, that's different because there's no real budget for it." And here is where tradition and technology cross paths; the new resin signs at $700 are more durable and cheaper than the $2,400 redwood signs. "Plus they look good," Jon says, "and everyone's glad the stenciling at the top is staying." The new signs no longer have fieldstone bases— they need to be crash resistant. One thing that hasn't changed is vandalism, weather, and misguided snowplows, all contributing to Jon's job security.

For the armchair traveler Jon has edited *Montana's Historical Highway Markers,* which puts the redwood signs in your lap. But there are pages waiting to be written—Jon has his eye on future sites. "I'd like to see a sign in Columbus marking two concrete buildings that were built prior to

World War I. They're the prototypes of hollow wall construction and were built when the patent was applied for." Today most people pass by the derelict buildings without even noticing them or realizing their historical value. Behind them is the yard where stone was cut for the blocks in the state capitol—even more reason to put up a marker. The other place he'd like to have marked is a missile silo somewhere in Montana, recording the cold war, but "I haven't approached the Feds about it yet—they may not be too keen on it."

If you really want another round of beer with this guy, ask him about the state's bridges—there aren't many he hasn't crossed, but he quickly admits that going over some of the old ones gives him the creeps. Even the locals have a love-hate relationship with their bridges—they hate driving them but for aesthetic and nostalgic reasons don't want to see them replaced. Almost reverently, Jon says, "They're a part of engineering and Montana's history; different eras are identified by the type of construction and techniques." When construction projects interfere, he determines why a bridge should be saved, then tries to find a new owner for the massive white elephant.

Engineers and historians are often at odds, especially about the old bridges. Jon sees the engineers as more analytic and the historians as abstract and romantic. "Since 1990 only twice did the engineers get excited about saving a bridge." One such bridge, in Alberton, is partially supported by a natural rock formation in the middle of the river. The other is a unique pin-connected Pratt truss bridge in Augusta that Jon believes is the only one like it left in the United States.

For every bridge there's a story and for every story there's a sign. So the next time you're reading one and notice the guy in the car next to you staring, walk over and tell Jon how much you enjoy his work. ◆

It's not often you see the words *caviar* and *Montana* in the same sentence. But in Glendive fish eggs are big business. Bob Chelgren can tell you that the going rate for a three-ounce tin of this stuff from the Yellowstone River is $35. Considering that one ounce of roe fills a shot glass, that's pretty heady stuff at about $12 a shot. That may sound steep, but even the Russians know quality when they taste it and are passing over their own beluga for this delicacy harvested from paddlefish. As the official weigher and one of the select few caviar makers, Bob knows paddlefish inside and out.

"If it has anything to do with paddlefishing, I love it," he says. Give him a minute, or thirty, and he'll tell you more than you'll ever remember about the lunker. The biggest one Bob ever caught weighed 104 pounds but the record is 142.5. One female can produce up to 22 pounds of eggs, and "it's not necessarily the largest fish that yields the most eggs," he notes. Don't worry about choking on a bone—there aren't any, except for the jawbone, which can be read like tree rings—the oldest fish recorded is fifty-five years.

Some fish just for the meat, which when boiled and dunked in butter tastes like lobster.

These large fish with snouts like canoe paddles have been in the river for thousands of years. They were popular in the 1800s but died off, many people believing that they went extinct. So imagine the excitement when someone accidentally snagged one in the 1960s—through word of mouth a new craze was born. It took another thirty years until the chamber of commerce connected the dots: Paddlefish are related to sturgeon; sturgeon eggs are caviar; paddlefish eggs were going to waste. There was money to be made. Legal and financial details requiring a special permit to sell part of a game fish were worked out

PADDLEFISH CAVIAR EXPERT

BOB CHELGREN, GLENDIVE

between the chamber and Fish and Game, and even the governor approved. In the Paddlefish Capital of the World, who better to run the program than a fisherman, so Bob agreed when the chamber approached him to be site foreman at Intake, command central for egg outtake.

The six-week season isn't a free-for-all, and Bob makes sure it stays that way. "In 1991 the fish were so thick in the river that you could see ten or twelve fishermen at a time coming toward the weigh station with their catch in hand," he says. Through the frenzy he checks that every fish is properly tagged and each fisherman follows the rules. "You have to fish from shore, no throwing back for a larger catch, and you can't pass your pole off to someone else," he warns. That's so strictly enforced that there are stories about parents tying their kids to trees to prevent them from being yanked into the river. Poles are rigged with a special heavy-duty line, and some use an old spark plug as the suggested five-ounce sinker.

The scales are state regulated. Bob recalls more than one angler who tried for a record by adding rocks: "Of course we find them when we clean the fish." The process is simple: A fish is brought to the cleaning station—not an easy task when you're lugging something the size of your little brother—where volunteers clean it for free in exchange for the eggs (legally they can't charge for the service). Fishermen may clean their own and keep the eggs, but it's a messy job and caviar prep is tricky. "The average fisherman can't process the caviar properly, so there's no incentive to keep the eggs. Even if they did, they aren't allowed to sell them."

Eggs break down quickly and turn to mush, so the fish need to be cleaned right away. Here fish cleaning has become somewhat of a spectator sport, with more than a few folks engrossed at the sight of gray-green eggs being separated from their gooey membranes as they're forced through a mesh screen. But only a select few—Bob among them—are privy to the caviar-making process, which like the formula for Coca-Cola is top secret. "It's a special recipe, which basically boils down to the kind of salt and the amount used," he notes. Each little ovum is then herded into a walk-in cooler, home for the next three to five weeks. Bob adds, "They need to age before they're really good; in fact we ship them frozen—it doesn't hurt them."

Demand for Yellowstone caviar is worldwide. It's especially popular in Japan and New York, where it enjoys celebrity as holiday fare. The eggs are sorted and packed by color, and for the price, one would think they'd look more festive, but the average buyer prefers dark gray. A lot of the eggs are sold to wholesalers, who "mark it up a lot," according to Bob, "but the chamber gets its share, more than $1 million since the program began. Nearly 100 percent of the fishermen participate. We don't charge to clean the male fish but always hope for a donation." Every little bit helps. Historical, educational, and recreational organizations vie for the grant money created by the sale of caviar. Fish and Game uses its share for upgrading parks and further fish study. Money also goes to improving the campground at Intake Diversion Dam, official weigh-in site.

People come from hundreds of miles for paddlefishing, and Glendive is the perfect host. The first fish of the season nets the lucky angler a special cap and laminated photo—now there's an incentive. Success has its imitators, and Bob is proud to point out that his program has been a model for North Dakota. "There's even one fellow who made boots and belts out of paddlefish hide— it's tough stuff. I don't know that it will catch on as well as the eggs," he chuckles, "but then again we were throwing them away for years, too." ✦

The next time you drive past a grain elevator—any of the hundreds in Montana—you can be pretty sure Bruce Selyem has been there. He gives a whole new meaning to the term *drive-by shooting:* He's a grain elevator photographer. What began as a mild interest has become a full-blown obsession, a way of life. Pull into his driveway, the one with a mailbox and doghouse shaped like a grain elevator, and you know these folks are a little different; then step inside and enter a showcase, a private museum of sorts, of every aspect of these grain buildings. Framed elevator photos—239 in all, most of them shot by Bruce—cover nearly every inch of wall space. The elevator theme is everywhere: scale models, clocks, a chess set, a cribbage board, and cases of ephemera that include an 1890s McKinley hankie with, of course, an elevator on it.

It's hard to believe that there was a time when Bruce didn't know what a grain elevator

GRAIN ELEVATOR PHOTOGRAPHER

BRUCE SELYEM, BOZEMAN

was. The first one he photographed, near his home in Bozeman, he labeled simply as "building." He had no idea that this photo of the Anceney elevator would be the first of 63,000 (and counting), all cataloged on his computer, and all his favorites.

While growing up in East Glacier, Bruce photographed mostly landscapes and wildflowers, but he wanted a degree in photography, which brought him to Montana State University. As staff photographer for the Museum of the Rockies, he traveled the state documenting the museum's dino digs. During his forays he took a closer look at these prairie skyscrapers and, now knowing what that Anceney building was, he decided hey, why not photograph every one in Montana. Little did he realize that the two hundred photos he shot that first year were a drop in the bucket (in 2001 he took ten thousand photos). When he returned to shoot places in better lighting and found them torn down, he felt he had to do something about it, so he formed the Country Grain Elevator Historical Society, a nonprofit organization to preserve the history of these structures. When his job at the museum was phased out, Bruce had the time he wanted to track down more elevators.

When people ask how he knows if he's photographed them all, Bruce whips out a beat-up atlas and an old railroad map that pinpoints each elevator. "The railroad has had a huge impact on the elevators; it's the reason the buildings were put there in the first place, and because they've become a liability, the reason they're being torn down," he explains. So, for three to four months a year, he and his wife, Barbara, hit the road with a crate of yellow highlighters, racking up 25,000 to 40,000 miles in the United States and Canada. Their atlas has so many towns marked in yellow there's barely any discernible background left on the pages.

Barbara isn't along just for the ride. She heads off to track down the building's history, whether from a local farmer—the best source—or the employees of a still-operating facility, as Bruce sets up his tripod. "At their peak there were twenty-seven thousand in the United States," he says, "four hundred in Montana alone, and six thousand in Canada—even Alaska still has five." The older buildings are wood, some of which are sided with metal for fire protection, a common threat when you mix dry prairie with moving trains. Many are white, but red was popular as well because it was especially cheap paint back then. Paint is not a factor today because the older ones are being replaced by concrete monstrosities. Bruce adds, "The building's distinctive shape is because of the conveyor in the smaller top segment. Their footprint averages 30 by 32 feet, and older elevators can hold thirty thousand bushels of grain." Pretty impressive from someone who didn't even know what these things were a few years ago.

After visiting more than thirty-two hundred sites, he says his biggest concerns are skunks and nails, although there was that snake incident. After trying to chase a coiled-up rattler by throwing his tripod at it, he was left with a coiled up rattler and no tripod. With no rocks in sight, he resorted to Montana ingenuity, tossing cow pies at the critter until it moved off. But it was a human encounter on a shoot in California that almost sent him to that big grain elevator in the sky. He was attacked by a deranged man wielding an 8-foot pipe, which led to a wrestling match in the mud. In the end Bruce got the shot.

His are not run-of-the-mill snapshots—they're fine art. Besides power lines, adjacent buildings, or general clutter, Bruce's biggest problem in getting the perfect shot is Dumpsters: "They're big, brightly painted, and always in the worst possible spot." Once he has the best angle nailed down, there's the problem of lighting. More than once, to be there for the perfect morning light, Bruce has thrown down his sleeping bag and shared the inside of an elevator with its resident birds and mice and the wind. But he's not complaining: "I like the wind—it tells stories of the elevator. It's OK that I don't know what it's saying."

Bruce's goal is to eventually find an affordable elevator in the right location for a museum and headquarters for the society. In the meantime he's content to promote the organization and generate memberships at grain conventions, through magazine articles, and with the occasional radio interview. His photos, which have graced magazine covers, are on display through a traveling exhibit as well as on his Web site (www.grainelevatorphotos .com, with a link to the society site).

Life for Bruce is one big grain elevator; in fact, if it weren't for these pieces of Americana, he might still be a bachelor, because it was through his contact with a grain magazine that he met Barbara. Like true devotees, they were even married in a grain elevator—the "building" at Anceney. ◆

Dressed in her Sunday best and leaning against her aluminum walker for stability, Blanche Harding waves her arms in jerky but deliberate motions. Her body is slightly hunched over; her voice takes on a dramatically different personality. In the Polson-Flathead Historical Museum a small crowd has gathered to watch. Her arthritic hands deftly manipulate the control paddles and strings that bring Meriwether Lewis—a wooden marionette—to life. Standing 27 inches, nearly half Blanche's height, the jointed Lewis nods and bows on cue. And even in today's high-tech, special-effects world, everyone around her is engrossed. But then, everything about Blanche is engrossing.

Raised in North Dakota, she did the usual little-girl things, playing with paper dolls and putting on shows for her friends, often making up scenes as she went along. "I had a shoe holder for a stage, and I'd make the dolls part of fairy tales,"

PUPPETEER

BLANCHE HARDING, POLSON

she says. "To be realistic, I'd take on a different voice for each one. It was such fun." But of course, she grew up and temporarily traded her puppets for college.

Blanche loves to spin a good yarn, especially about how she met her husband. He was an industrial arts teacher at the University of North Dakota, where she was a sophomore speech major thirteen years his junior. "I was immediately taken by him and his good looks—and wanted to take one of his classes desperately so I could be close to him." When she found out he also taught mechanical drawing, she signed up—apparently the only girl to do so. One day he kept her after class and she asked him what she had done wrong. He told her it was difficult to teach with her around. Blanche grins, "Then I knew I had him." Sound devious? Not for her. This determined lady knew what she wanted and went after it.

Summers found them in Polson, at their home on Indian Bay. Although they both taught full-time, Blanche always had puppets in the back of her mind. She recalls seeing her first marionette performance—*Noah's Ark*—and fell in love with the concept. She went back for a second show hoping to get a behind-the-scenes look at how it was done, and knowing they would ask for volunteers to "feed" one of the animals, she sat up front. Blanche stops reminiscing just long enough to demonstrate how to create a face with her hand—her thumb a lower jaw chewing.

"I thought it would be such fun to put on my own shows, but I never imagined it would happen the summer I worked as a cook in Glacier Park. I was known for my apple pies but I loved the chance to teach kids something different," mainly with her handcrafted tap puppets, wooden figures on a stick that she would make dance by tapping the board resting in her lap. Quick to capitalize on a hot market, she and her young son sold several hundred that year in the park for $2.00 each. As business grew, so did their craft. They painted them fancier and dressed them as cowboys, with kerchiefs and hats.

Back in school she took on the persona of grade school teacher, with teachers' aides no kid could resist—puppets. "The girls always wanted to be the princess but sometimes you have to be the bad man—that's where the acting comes in." Soon Blanche took her shows on the road, performing all over Montana and North Dakota. As a greenhorn she charged $10 to put on a show, but as she became more advanced, her fee went to $50, with contracts signed in advance and a backlog of bookings. "I was having a ball."

Puppeteering made her more aware of people's accents, which she would remember for different characters in her plays. Her education as a speech major paid off: "How you stress a word can change its meaning. You can say 'oh' with surprise, sorrow, or inquisitiveness—so many ways. You need to know that if you're going to be a puppeteer."

Talking like a puppet is only half the act—Blanche also had to know how to make them. Since there was no Toys"R"Us, she did the next best thing and made her own, cutting body parts on a band saw: "Basswood is ideal for puppets because it's heavy and there are no knots—a finished marionette can weigh fifteen pounds." And of course it wouldn't do to have a naked puppet, so she sewed their costumes as well. Blanche explains, "I used chamois for rawhide because it's softer and more pliable. I sculpted the head from a putty that dried hard as wood and added real hair if I could get it." To finish them off, she hand-painted their faces and then strung the parts together with heavy thread she coerced from a local shoemaker. And when her script had President Jefferson invite Clark to "come in and have a chair," she realized she needed to make furniture, too.

Without a script you have unemployed puppets, so Blanche set about putting her characters to work. When most folks are thinking of retiring to warmer climates, at ninety-four she wrote the script for the Lewis and Clark story. "It has everything a good tale needs: a hero, a villain, a woman, and a dog." She did loads of research to get her facts straight: "You couldn't call it a reservation—they didn't exist then; it was Indian country."

Blanche made many puppets in her lifetime, but little did she know she was crafting folk art heirlooms. She even paid a lawyer's fee with one—his choice. Her children have some; others are in museums in North Dakota and Wyoming and of course here in Polson, where there's a special display of her Lewis and Clark characters.

As Blanche finishes the demonstration, she gently lays down her puppet. The crowd disperses satisfied, knowing they have seen something special. ✦

With the ranch work done and the sun setting behind Lemhi Pass, Sandy James grabs his violin case, hops into his pickup, and drives the 40 miles from Horse Prairie Valley to his second home in Dillon. The Village People's "Macho Man" runs through his head as he pictures their album propped where he left it on the piano, a far cry from the classics his mom played on her Steinway.

As a youngster on the family ranch, which he still runs, music was a fact of life. Dad put aside his music degree to manage the spread but had musical hopes for his son and surrounded him with big-band sounds and show tunes. "My parents had a big body of musical work for me to revolt against," Sandy chuckles. Instead, he was drawn to the country-and-western sounds he absorbed hanging around the bunkhouse with the ranch hands.

Sandy never had early formal musical training—he didn't even play in the school band—

FIDDLER

SANDY JAMES, DILLON

---

so it was with some surprise that at the age of fourteen he bought a player piano, all because of a cow. His father felt sorry for him when Sandy lost his prize 4-H steer, so for a buck he sold the boy his Jeep, which Sandy traded for a '47 Chevy, then sold the car to buy the piano from a family who had to leave their home when Clark Canyon Reservoir was created. Now he was content to sit at home, pumping the piano while accompanying himself on the clarinet.

A few years later, during a summer break from college, he found a couple of old banjos in the attic back at the ranch. Sandy began plucking. In 1976 he decided to make mastering the fiddle his bicentennial project. "I was nearly thirty and figured if I didn't do it now it was never going to happen," he recalls. About that time the state prison guards went on strike, and as part of the National Guard, Sandy was called up to help out. He used his time there to fine-tune his skills and enjoys telling people he learned to play by ear "while I was in prison." Always looking to improve, he found an instructor in Dillon who could help and soon after joined the Montana Old Time Fiddlers Association.

In 1981 the Dillon Junior Fiddlers Association was formed to encourage young fiddlers, and the town got behind it, sponsoring the U.S. Open Old-Time Fiddlers' Contest. When his instructor left, Sandy filled the void and soon had his own fold of future fiddlers. As musical directors for the group, he and his wife, Jeannie, created a program for the kids to take on the road. Montana's centennial provided the perfect opportunity, and Jeannie wrote "Rosin Up the Bow," a lighthearted historical musical revue that needed forty kids and sixty costumes. Sandy says, "Initially, ten of the kids played the right notes, and it required some highly creative microphone management. By the time we produced the show, the kids were playing well." The show toured to standing ovations.

In spite of the fiddling frenzy developing in southwestern Montana, the contest wasn't paying its way and was discontinued, until the Junior Fiddlers stepped in and took over. Today it's a popular venue for aficionados who arrive each February, fiddle in hand, from throughout the West, eager to play traditional fiddle favorites.

But not Sandy. "Ode to Martha Stewart"—hardly a Gershwin tune—is a Sandy James original. This triple-threat guy—writer, musician, singer—is jamming with son Owen, on the violin, playing to a before-dinner group in the parlor. In marked contrast to his laid-back, unassuming personality, he hammers the keyboard while belting out his satire on the queen of craft. Jeannie requests her favorite, "Prozac and Viagra," and he doesn't miss a beat as he segues from insider trading to erectile dysfunction. "Now Granny said her sugar and spice was few and far between / Til she started putting Viagra in Granddad's Ovaltine / Now they're acting just like newlyweds / What's even more, she said / When he's asleep, it keeps him / From rolling out of bed." Knowing they'd play until midnight, Jeannie interrupts to announce dinner, but it's still another fifteen minutes before they wind down.

The James family has talent to spare, and Sandy is the driving force behind their music. Sandy, Owen, and daughter Amy have been crowned Montana state fiddle champions; Jeannie pens scripts, makes costumes, and joins in on the cello. They have a trailer of gear packed and ready and often choose the music on the way to the venue. To paraphrase an old vaudeville line, Sandy says, "We perform for anybody, from the crowned heads of Europe to the county seats of Montana." He plunks down several photo albums to make his point, spreading out their fiddling history in front of him, from performing in New York City to their float in the Fourth of July parade in Washington, D.C. But most prized are the pictures of their trips to Japan, one as part of an entourage of Montanans sent to enhance trade relations and a year later one with the entire Junior Fiddlers, who were invited to perform at the Kumamoto Youth Music Festival. Sandy smiles as he remembers school groups singing "Home on the Range" in Japanese and says he would like to create a similar program to take to Scotland.

Until then he has his hands full researching and arranging the music for historical balls. "The music and the costumes must fit the period," he says. What began with the grand Centennial Ball in the Senate chambers in Helena has progressed to the Custer reenactment ball in Hardin, the Grand Ball of 1864 in Virginia City, and their latest, the Titanic Ball, featuring ragtime music.

Back in the pickup with Horse Prairie Valley in his sights, Sandy hums, then lightly taps on the steering wheel, making a mental note to get this ditty down on paper, but it will probably stay in his head with the others, at least until the next gig. ◆

It takes Olen Raisland just over two minutes to transform a fluffy, robust-looking sheep into something resembling a poster child for the wool industry. That's one down and 27,999 to go. So begins another season of sheepshearing for Olen and his crew. Since the mid-1970s he's carried on the family tradition that his grandfather began in the 1930s and that Olen learned by practicing on the family dog. Situated north of Reedpoint in the heart of sheep country, Olen's ranch is 1,272 acres of some of the prettiest land in the state, but he's not home much to enjoy it. While the rest of us are indoors for the winter, snuggled in wool blankets and wool clothing, he's out on the road, shears and equipment in hand.

His busiest time of year is from December through spring, but he's far from idle in summer. As much as technology has improved his job, it's still hot, dirty, backbreaking work. On a July afternoon at a ranch in Belgrade, the still, hot air of the barn is alive with pesky flies, bleating, squirming sheep, and the buzz of three sets of clippers. The sheep are in a chute lined up like railroad cars, waiting to be plucked through one of three doors to land center stage. One man wrestles with a two-hundred-pound pregnant ewe, positioning it on the floor between his legs to control it. Olen notes, "It's better to shear before lambing. When sheep lamb out it causes a fever and a break in the wool and changes the consistency, which makes it tougher to cut." Olen skillfully shears a year's worth of the dirtier belly wool from another animal and lays it aside on the lesser-grade pile.

Looking up from his work, he says, "We want to cut as close as possible to the skin but don't want to tear up the fleece," then turns back to his victim. He shears in a pattern to create one big chunk, yielding a single fleece. The barnyard chickens look on as the twelve pounds of fluff are gathered and stuffed into a nearby baler. Without

SHEEPSHEARER

OLEN RAISLAND, REEDPOINT

hesitating, Olen releases this bemused sheep and reaches for the next.

The bulk of the shearing is done seven days a week from February through April. Of course Olen can't do it all himself, so he contracts out for a team of two to six helpers. Off peak they're usually busy spot shearing, "removing eye wool—it blocks their vision—and clearing their butt and getting rid of dingleballs for breeding." He packs up his camper and travels a circuit that takes him from Deer Lodge to Dillon to Conrad, 20,000 miles by season's end. "Without my wife, Bobbi's, help at home tending chores and dealing with daily problems, I don't think I could continue to shear on the road. She's my partner," Olen says.

Although each stop has its challenges, few things are worse than wet sheep. Wet woolen socks might keep our feet warm, but a wet sheep can make the shearer ill with "wool pneumonia." Olen says, "We wear wool if we know we're going to be shearing wet stock; we're wet but we're warm."

Dampness doesn't do much for the wool, either; it mildews.

Olen shears nine thousand to ten thousand sheep a year by himself—a far cry from the forty-seven head it took him two days to do when he was in high school. It's not that he aspired to follow in his father's footsteps: "I did them because Dad hurt his back and needed help. I got 75 cents a head." Sheep raising is labor-intensive. "Fewer people are doing it; it's down to the diehards." These days he gets paid more but smiles and says, "It all goes into the black hole, also known as my ranch." Because he raises his own sheep, he's familiar with both sides of the business—selling and shearing.

The number of shearing jobs drops each year. Ranchers have to deal with predators, drought, imported wool, and sheep disease, which, he says is "a catchall term for sheep that seem to die for no reason." Olen has to compete with seasonal New Zealanders who come here for jobs.

Synthetics have also had a negative impact on the wool industry, but the military still uses wool for uniforms, and Pendleton blankets will most likely always be a wool staple. Like most ranchers, Olen sells his fleeces to a wool pool. "They've even pooled with other pools," he notes. Then the wool is graded. (Black-face wool is less valuable because the black hairs can't be dyed.) The best grades are combined into one lot, hoping that larger lots will attract bigger buyers. Now the wool fetches a rancher up to $1.00 a pound for top-of-the-line grade, but Olen still charges by the head.

Although Olen is a third-generation sheepshearer (his older brother shears, too), his work is just a bit easier than when his father and grandfather were in business. Electric clippers have replaced the manual shears that were sharpened to perfection: "Granddad could make a blow with one pass, like scissors through paper." A baling machine, electric fans, and back-support braces make shearing more tolerable, but Olen still puts in a long day. And without modern prescription creams, he'd have to find another line of work—he's allergic to the lanolin in the wool, putting to rest the myth that all sheepshearers have soft hands. Instead, he breaks out, itches, and wears gloves and long-sleeved shirts on even the hottest days.

Come Labor Day weekend Olen gets in his pickup and heads 10 miles east, to the Reedpoint Sheep Drive, where as one of the main attractions he demonstrates the fine art of shearing to festivalgoers, who often have no idea where sweaters come from.

They watch, entranced, unaware that what Olen makes look effortless is actually years of experience and sheep know-how. He says, "You need to think like a sheep and then you can work with them." ◆

Western memorabilia overruns his home office, where an autographed Roy Rogers jigsaw puzzle fights for precious space with rodeo posters, cowboy garb, and related ephemera. A horse-head tie rack holds his collection of vintage neckties adorned with hand-painted ponies and bronc riders. Ashtrays, lamps, shoot-'em-up movie stills— there's barely room for the manual Smith Corona that he prefers over a computer. A bumper sticker above the door sums up this cowboy poet's philosophy. It reads KEEP IT WILD—a motto Paul Zarzyski says he borrowed from the Montana Wilderness Association. He states emphatically, passionately, "It—that all-encompassing pronoun—the West, the poetry, the cowboy, the land, the open range, the animals— keep it *all* wild."

"If you want to label me, call me 'the one and only Polish-hobo-rodeo-poet of Manchester, Montana [so far]'—I wear the cowboy poet badge

COWBOY POET

PAUL ZARZYSKI, GREAT FALLS

with great honor," he says. But he wasn't always a fan of verse—for a while he hated it. As a kid growing up in Wisconsin, he enjoyed poetry until teachers "made us find the DHM (deeper hidden meaning) and ruined it for us. Every time I tried to understand poets, I'd get an F." The turning point came in college when, rather than study for an organic chemistry test, he wrote "Zarzyski, Not Exactly Wild Bill Hickok," a poem about his frustrations with duck hunting. "I got the lowest test score in class," he brags.

His biggest influence was a professor who also happened to be a renegade poet. "He did something no other teacher did; he gave me complete literary freedom," notes Paul. Before long Paul's two great loves, poetry and Montana, merged and he became a master of multitasking— teaching, writing poetry, and working the rodeo circuit as a bronc rider. "I love rodeo people and that genre," but this style of poetry isn't limited to cowboys or western themes. Paul says there are two kinds of cowboy poets: "Those who are cowboys and write poetry and those who are poets and write about cowboys." He considers himself the latter.

Why cowboy and not mining, lumberjacking, or huntin' poets? Paul surmises that in the late 1800s, cowboys on long cattle drives had lots of thinking time and conjured up poems they'd memorize, then share over evening campfires. Cowboy poetry exists because a few actually wrote down their poems, which were published. Back then the poems told the story of the working cowboy—today, anything goes.

Just like country-and-western music, which Paul feels has not changed for the better, cowboy poetry is always in a state of flux. He likes cowboy poetry for its ability to get the story told without having to find the DHM. "I have roughly one hundred poems in my head that I can recite," he says, and launches into an excerpt from "Why I Like Butte." He enunciates and punctuates his words with a Wisconsin twang that thirty years in Montana haven't been able to erase:

. . . BUTTE! the one and only

arena I did not bite the dirt in—never

dusted, pile-drived, or drilled—where I prayed

Hail Marys long before the Mountaintop

Madonna, *Our Lady of the Rockies,* the Butte Guadalupe,

beamed down upon the buckin' chutes—

prayed the same *Hail Mary*

full of grace I pleaded as a child wanting

to be spared a lifetime in the mines. BUTTE! . . .

Paul quotes from his mentor, Richard Hugo: "If you want to become a poet, first learn to have fun with the sounds of words." But sometimes Paul is faced with the sound of silence when he draws a blank during an onstage performance. If it's a familiar classic poem, audience members yell out the words; if not, Paul calmly tells them, "I'll recite that one at the bar for you later." And that's just fine with the crowd.

Paul's life partner, Liz, was instrumental in launching the granddaddy of all cowboy poetry gatherings, in Elko, Nevada, in the early 1980s. Up to ten thousand fans annually attend this "Cowpoke Woodstock," which according to Paul is like a big family reunion "except everyone gets along." Since then other states have joined in and now similar gatherings are in major cities nationwide. The big event in Montana takes place in Lewistown. Paul says the introduction—he gets to come out on the stage and deliver one of his poems—is similar to the thrill of sitting in the rodeo chute on a bronc: "an incredible rush."

Because he's tagged a cowboy poet, he's invited to some events as a novelty. That doesn't bother him, and in fact he likes to use the opportunity to "take their stereotype and blow it to smithereens." He cites, for example, "Shoes," a powerful piece he wrote after viewing an exhibit at the Holocaust Museum. Although he writes in traditional rhyme, it's his free verse that sets him apart from other cowboy poets and gets him invited back repeatedly.

Like the cowboys before him, Paul has written it all down, producing a number of smaller poetry books, two CDs, and his latest and largest effort, a sixty-poem tome titled *Wolf Tracks on the Welcome Mat*. (Much more about Paul and his work can be found at the Western Folk Life Center Web site [www.westernfolklife.org].)

"I'm lucky to be doing something I love so much," Paul remarks as he steps onto the stage. A spotlight catches highlights from his cowboy hat. The audience is silent, anticipating his words, ready to help out if needed. He brushes a piece of lint off his trademark 1940s kitsch necktie, and in a distinctive Midwest accent, begins . . . ◆

Every August the population of Crow Agency explodes as thousands of visitors come to Crow Fair, appropriately christened "the tepee capital of the world." Hundreds of the white structures dot the landscape, except for one. Peggy White's is bright blue and yellow and stands out from all the rest, as does its owner.

Just down the road in Garryowen facing the interstate stands a mishmash of buildings, Peggy's compound of sorts, where a sign at the entrance greets visitors: SHO DAU CHEI, Crow for "hello." It's one of the hottest days on record but people are busy everywhere, seemingly oblivious to the blistering sun, intent on their mission to add yet another building. Like several others, this one is made of straw bales, unique on the reservation but only a part of what visitors find here.

Peggy is eager to give the tour, trying to show everything at once, and you almost have to run to keep up with her. She points out the chil-

NATIVE AMERICAN ENTREPRENEUR

PEGGY WHITE, GARRYOWEN

dren's house, a safe house "where children go to wipe their tears," she says. A donated old mobile home serves as a food bank, run like most everything else on the property by volunteers. Peggy raised money for one month's food dispersal by selling pumpkins from her pickup and proudly adds, "We gave out forty thousand pounds of meat in one year." Next to the food bank another mobile home, the Buffalo Nickel Thrift Shop, is chock-full of clothing that Peggy and her crew hand out to whoever needs it: "We don't care if it's whites or Indians; anyone is welcome to it," a point she makes about everything on the property. There's also a library loaded with books, many waiting to be cataloged.

The heart of the complex is straw bales, which have gotten a lot of attention since she put up her first building. It all began through a group in Virginia, the Kelly Foundation, which was responsible for Peggy's son going to college. At the time Peggy had no house, living instead in a run-down trailer on family land. After researching straw bale houses, she had a road, electricity, septic, and a well put in, then dealt with governmental bureaucracy and the Bureau of Indian Affairs. Peggy asked for help from the University of Washington, Penn State, and the American Indian Housing Initiative, and soon her house became reality, a guinea pig.

Peggy says, "You can't use any old bale of straw; it has to be baled just right or it falls apart." Her house is made up of six hundred bales stacked two deep, creating a nearly 4-foot-thick wall that's stuccoed. The R-70 insulation rating is more than twice that of an average two-by-six studded house. Doubting Thomases are encouraged to open the small door on the wall in the dining room, where the view is anything but breathtaking—it's a window to the straw bales inside. The first concern that pops into most people's minds is fire danger, but Peggy assures that "no oxygen can get to the straw, so it can't burn."

Although hers wasn't the first in Montana, it was a first for the reservation. The best straw bales they could find came from Washington, but at $6.75 each, construction was expensive. Their next project, the WellKnown Buffalo (named for her grandmother) Cultural Center, used cheaper local bales at $2.75 and pole construction, with the idea that it would be more affordable for reservation residents. Peggy has learned by doing and now teaches potential homeowners straw bale construction; she says it instills pride of ownership to have them help with building. After building her house, the Center Pole Foundation was established as a nonprofit organization to help others.

The main building—WellKnown Buffalo Cultural Center (www.wellknownbuffalo.com)—is bustling with workers putting a layer of cement on the straw bale walls. This space is for budding entrepreneurs to sell their handiwork through the *A Wa Ku Leh,* the Little People's Trading Post; acquire computer skills; learn a traditional craft; or dine on Native American food—"We serve elk, deer, and buffalo"— and take turns with their latest acquisition, a coffee roaster. Every gift shop in Crow country has coffee, but not like Peggy's. Her special blend uses bitterroot "for good feelings and clear expression," according to its label, and St. John's-wort, "gathered at the Bighorn Battlefield." Like all of Peggy's projects, profits go toward educating Native American youth.

The actual center pole for the cultural building is from the Bighorn Mountains, installed in a special ceremony and blessed by a sun dance chief. Peggy says that the "center pole in Crow culture gives strength, guidance, and it's where you go for help. It connects you to heaven to *a bada di,* the creator." Everything Peggy does is spiritual (at eighteen she was given the gift of traditional healing from her great-grandmother). "The Little People are mystical beings of Crow tradition that live in the Pryor Mountains," she says, explaining the play on words for the Little People's Trading Post. "They're hardworking just like our students. You'll have good fortune if you see one."

Peggy's complex is a work in progress. She welcomes anyone to use her sweat lodge for "cleansing and purifying" or the tepee for an overnight stay. She'll gladly arrange a week's worth of activities for those who want to stay longer. There are plans for a museum, and an amphitheater is being built for "kids to reenact their history." Peggy wants the youth to empower themselves and pass on their culture. "The worst thing is to be hopeless and helpless with no trade, no education, and poor health care. We're Americans but we're not. The more I can teach the nonnatives, the better for our children."

Like a traditional Crow home, the entrance to Peggy's faces east to greet the morning sun. From her doorway she can see the Bighorn Battlefield, about a half mile away. As visitors leave, Peggy gives the customary farewell: *Kun naa dii waá a chiilii*—"May you have many more good days." *Aho* (thank you). ◆

There was the truck incident. Or as Charles calls it, "the 8.5 hours God gave me to reflect on my life." It was a cold February day in 2000 out on the range southeast of Broadus, just weeks after he had broken his hip when his horse went down on the ice. Insisting it was just a crack, the sixty-eight-year-old rancher didn't see a doctor, and his hip was the last thing on his mind as he hopped into the back of his pickup to pitch hay to his cat- tle—throttle cocked open to a creep and steering wheel tied in place, which he often did when there was no one around to help. But for some reason still unknown to Charles, as the vehicle plodded along, his feet went out from under him and he landed squarely on the same hip—this time undeniably broken. More than once he tried to get up but passed out from the pain. As he watched his truck happily chug off toward the horizon, he knew his only choice was to wait it out until someone realized he was missing. He

---

COWBOY

CHARLES PATTEN, BROADUS

---

tucked a frozen cow pie under his head and gazed at the winter sky. After some time in deep thought and agony, his concentration was interrupted by the sound of an approaching vehicle. Rescue, he hoped, but quickly realized it was his own truck. "The damn thing had turned itself around and was aimed toward me and I couldn't do a thing but watch." It rolled near him, then surprisingly stopped, and "damned if the radio didn't come on by itself and start playing music." If any- one else were to tell you the story, you'd have seri- ous doubts about its veracity, but it's typical Charles Patten.

The product of homesteaders, Charles (never Charlie) is the quintessential cowboy. You hear it in his language, feel it in his voice, see it in his weathered face. He got his first ranching expe- rience working on his parents' spread, where he encountered various rough string riders (freelance cowboys of a sort who lived with the ranchers).

"They ate a million meals at my mother's table and taught me how to get a cow in, break a bronc, and the finer points of driving cattle. I learned more history from them than I got in school, too." He's plumb full of cowboy know-how: "Break a colt by corralling him overnight. By next morning he's so lonesome and happy for attention he won't buck you off." On driving cattle he stresses the importance of keeping calves and cows together. He pauses and reflects that "we had to learn modern ways—but try to keep the old ways alive."

When it came time to get his own place, he started with a band of sheep. These weren't easy times for ranchers, and Charles is visibly moved when he recalls those who helped him in so many ways, including financially: "I really miss the old guys." He eventually turned to cattle, forming the Patten Ranch Company, "held together initially with more welding rod and baling wire than anything." Managing two thousand Angus takes about one hundred thousand acres, and he did it with only a handful of employees. When the ranch was split up, Charles boasts that they sold one million pounds of feeder cattle in one season.

Ranchers know hardship—whether ravenous grasshoppers, drought, herd disease, or in Charles's case many broken bones. It's probably no surprise that during the local oil boom of the 1960s he took a shot at professional gambling. For nearly twenty years the Big Sky Bar was his home away from home, where he not only worked the tables but also was a bouncer—a tough old cuss who didn't mind getting in someone's face. Gambling and ranching seemed to work just fine—he managed the ranch every day and gambled until 2:00 A.M. Some nights weren't work at all—if customers were drunk enough, winning came easy. When the oil boom faded and gambling no longer paid, Charles moved on to yet another facet of the Old West—wagon trains.

For years he and his neighbors had been getting together for wagon train campfires. To celebrate Montana's centennial they took their prairie picnics on the road and formed a cattle drive. "We had three thousand head of cattle, including a number of longhorns, which added to the western feel, especially when their horns clanked when we ran the herd tight," Charles says. Cattle stretched for 1.5 miles, "which was really picturesque when they wound through the trees—a sight to behold, just like the old days."

The drive was so successful that it became a localized annual event, but events cost money, so they opened it up to paying guests. Since 1990 Charles and about ten families have operated the Powder River Cattle Drive (www.powderriver cattledrive.com). Even the hard-strapped Broadus business community liked the idea and chipped in $5,000 to get the train rolling.

It takes a lot of hard work to move eighty greenhorns and one hundred head of cattle 60 miles. Charles stresses that this cattle drive uses ranch horses, not trail horses that merely follow the leader: "Our guests need to learn how to ride and handle them." But all is not rough and tough—with portable toilets, showers, and a catering crew to dish up trail food these urban cowboys aren't far from civilization. For safety, cell phones are a necessity—but Charles laments, "these phones and mechanical stuff is changing things in ways that I don't really like to see."

It's a group effort, and although each guest forks over more than $1,000, it's hardly a money-maker. "It's a very small sideline. We don't do it for the money." Yet it's something they look forward to as much as the guests—great meals, a good dose of Charles's campfire tales, and lively music, for which they always hire a good band. "Some of them girls are so pretty, if I'd been dead less than three days, I'd get up and dance with them." ◆

His prayers were answered. Ordinarily that's the ending to a happy story. For Bob O'Bill, it was just the beginning. He's not an overly religious guy. "I haven't been to church in twenty-five years," he says. But when his wife, Joyce, became seriously ill, he prayed to the Lady of Guadalupe and promised to build a statue in the lady's honor if she recovered.

"I envisioned something like a 5-foot statue in the highlands south of Butte," he recalls. "But I woke up one morning and got inspired by the ridge as a site and started thinking larger—more like 60 feet." The final product, however, turned out to be nearly visible from space—the 90-foot-tall Our Lady of the Rockies, who looks down onto Butte from her perch on the Continental Divide. As the scope of the project grew, so did the manpower, and Bob can't emphasize enough that this was definitely not a one-man endeavor: "And it wasn't only men—the

women did as much as we did but they're not given much credit."

Twelve people sat in on the first meeting, one member suggesting a cross instead, but Bob's idea was as a tribute to women, and it stuck. To show his support, a merchant anted up $1,000 and another matched it. Some locals grumbled that the money could have been spent on more practical social and civic projects. In fact, very little money was used. Most people were enthused, and donations of time, material, and equipment poured in. Bob says, "We never really got turned down for anything. Like my son-in-law pointed out, it's like asking people if they want to help the Mother of God or not. What would you say?"

Although he's reluctant to take any credit for it, it's his favorite topic and he can talk about it for hours. The venture began in 1979 with Joyce's recovery and like any large-scale project involved

OUR LADY OF THE ROCKIES VISIONARY

BOB O'BILL, BUTTE

bureaucracy—lots of it. People wanted to help right away; however, Bob knew nothing could happen until they got the land. The property included a mining claim but Bob suggested purchasing just the surface rights. "Good thing, too, because later we were criticized for buying mining rights, which we hadn't."

Before they could move mountains, they had to plow through mounds of paperwork, and everyone from the EPA and Forest Service to the FAA had forms to be processed—yet it all happened with miraculous speed. For the first year a crew of four men and three kids volunteered their summer nights and weekends to create a crude road to the site, slowly and laboriously blasting and grading. "Some days we only made 10 feet of progress," Bob says. Over the next two years, the road was improved and the site was prepared. Bob made sure they were careful about how they cleared the area to keep their impact to a minimum: "When the EPA saw how clean it was, they were astonished. Because we hadn't done this

before, we figured this was how any land-conscious group would handle it."

The lady has gotten her share of knocks. Some wags say she's looking down with shame and sadness on the Berkley Pit. Ironically it's through the pit, the people who work there, and Bob's connection to it that she even exists. The pit's decline was her good fortune. Blasting materials, power drills, compressors, large construction equipment, and unemployed miners were available. When the pit sold its huge diesel-powered trucks, it first had to drain the fuel, and Bob claimed every drop. A visiting engineer told him it would take a ton of money to create the I beams for the statue's framework. Bob knew of a stockpile of industrial-grade pipe that the engineer said would work instead. The owner of the pipe said he couldn't just give it to Bob but he would sell him the whole works for the unheard-of price of $300. "I was speechless—I know the stuff runs $100 a foot."

The lady stands as tall as the Statue of Liberty. "Some wanted to go higher but 90 feet was the maximum the crane could handle," Bob notes. On December 20, 1985, six years after his prayer to Guadalupe, all work in Butte came to a standstill as supporters and critics alike watched a helicopter hoist the final piece into place.

Spotlights at the base illuminate her at night and, when the clouds are just right, create a halo. Bob laughs at how the FAA almost required them to put a flashing red light on top of her head. Even without the light, no planes have hit the lady, but she's had her share of lightning strikes—about one thousand annually. Every few years she gets a sprucing up with automotive paint—fitting, because her fingers are made of exhaust pipes.

Our Lady of the Rockies doesn't claim to have spiritual powers, but a few things have defied coincidence. During her recovery Joyce was given a 10-inch figure that was used as the model for the statue; its right hand broke. During the final assembly, the right hand on the lady was damaged when an uncharacteristic wind blew it into a nearby rock. Bob says, "In six years of construction, there was only one injury—a worker cut his right hand."

Tour buses wind their way up the forested 10-mile road, carrying the devoted, hopeful, and curious. Bob stresses that the lady is nondenominational and that the site is dedicated to all women. Visitors pile off the bus with photos of loved ones, stuffed animals, and other mementos to leave at the makeshift shrine within the statue's base. Inside, bulletin boards overflow with messages, and structural supports drip with rosaries.

When Bob's not working at the local food bank or helping Joyce tend to her herd of stray cats, you can find him hanging out with the other woman in his life. And if you're lucky, he just might be there when you step off the bus. ✦

If Lewis and Clark had known Scott Enloe, they would have traveled the Missouri River in style—lots of folks do. Instead of the crude pirogue they used to explore the West, they might have picked up a beauty at Scott's place in Great Falls. Just a couple of blocks off the big river, he makes canoes that border on fine art, "but they're meant to be used and are very durable," says Scott. "My son has more than 500 miles logged on his—he runs it over rocks and drags it onto shore."

Scott takes a deep breath before rattling off the litany of jobs that led him to canoe making. Fresh out of Montana State with a degree in music performance, he did what every struggling musician does: He roofed houses ("I had done one in high school, so I was 'qualified'"), washed dishes, worked as a teaching assistant, and delivered pizza. About the latter he notes: "There's some truth to the joke: 'How do you know when there's a trombone player at your door? Knock,

CANOE BUILDER

SCOTT ENLOE, GREAT FALLS

knock—Pizza Hut." Even worse, while in Las Vegas he went to a gathering of unemployed musicians that turned out to be an Amway party. He rolls his eyes: "I bought the starter kit." During a dishwashing gig in Ogden, Utah, he was hired by an insurance company that, in a roundabout way, landed him back in his hometown.

Every master craftsman has to start somewhere, so armed with only a screwdriver and a radial saw, he started knocking out family furniture "just for fun"—but it was hardly museum quality. "My first piece was a thrown-together nightstand that we still use," he says. "It was made of quarter-inch plywood and nailed together." Clearly, back then function came first.

Most likely Scott inherited his woodworking gene from his father. "I remember when Dad built a great boat from a set of plans out of *Popular Mechanics*," he says. That was probably in the back of Scott's mind when, seeing a shoddy canoe on a pickup, he decided he'd try to make one himself. "Besides," he adds, "they're easier to paddle down the river than a coffee table. I drove my friends nuts talking about making a wooden boat." He bought blueprints for his first project—a kayak—and pretty soon canoes filled his spare time as well as his garage. He and his wife, Beth, joined the local canoe club and signed up for a paddling class offered through the parks department. "They call it Marriage 101," he jokes, "but we're still married, and we learned a lot. You're supposed to kneel in a canoe," he points out, adding, "The Indians made the most stable water craft—the white man ruined it by adding seats."

In his garage workshop, Scott's Missouri River Boat Works is an evolution of his woodworking hobby. Floating masterpieces begin with either a trip to a small local lumber store or an e-mail to Canada to get mahogany, cedar strips, and boatbuilder's plywood. As Scott describes the construction process, he begins to speak in tongues: "I start with the bulkhead, then move on to the deck and portage yoke, which must be perfectly balanced. The gunwales are not only decorative, they're also structural and functional." This translates to mean he builds the frame first. Three-quarter-inch cedar strips 16 feet long are attached to the frame with glue and "clamped to death," then sealed to seaworthiness with fiberglass. "Cedar is one of the best things you can use," he says, "but it has a high silicon content, which is hard on bits and even harder on the lungs."

Scott's power tools collect dust while scrapers, sandpaper, and hand planes are put to use during the two hundred hours he's hunched over a project. A good part of that time is spent fussing over intricate designs and fitting alternating pieces of colored wood to form the final look that is distinctively Scott's. "When I'm finished I want a canoe that's not only functional but lightweight," he says, "no more than fifty-five pounds." He doesn't sign them—yet: "I feel my design and workmanship, especially on the decks, is my signature."

A canoe is almost useless without a paddle, so Scott makes them, too, but admits his first ones were fodder for the woodstove. After two years of refining the design, he has a paddle that's both pretty and functional. He considers himself a boat maker, but he's shooting for boatwright—"a boatbuilder who's lost count of the number of boats he's made."

Scott knows that not everyone can afford one of his finished canoes. Although fiberglass and aluminum are cheaper, there's something about the feel and character of a wooden boat that Sears can't supply. Knowing that Montana's long winters are perfect for the do-it-yourselfer, he began to offer canoes and kayaks in kit form for a fraction of the price of a finished one. The resulting popularity of the kits allowed Scott to give the insurance business the heave-ho so he could devote more time to marketing and customer relations. "I get e-mails from customers who send me photos of the boats they've made from my kits, and I post photos of my canoe trips on my Web site [www.scottsboatworks.com]," he says. "I love it; it's a very social thing."

He holds a course for Boy Scouts, who pack his garage to learn the fine art of making a plywood craft that's called the six-hour boat. "I'd like to offer adult classes, too," he says, but time's an issue. He's busy exhibiting his canoes and furniture—he's gotten better at that since his nightstand days—at art shows like the Charlie Russell.

It's a shame Lewis and Clark never met Scott; after all, they went right past his place—twice. They could have floated the Missouri in a custom-made craft that would have wowed the locals. But then again, it was a government project—they probably would have bought one of the kits. ◆

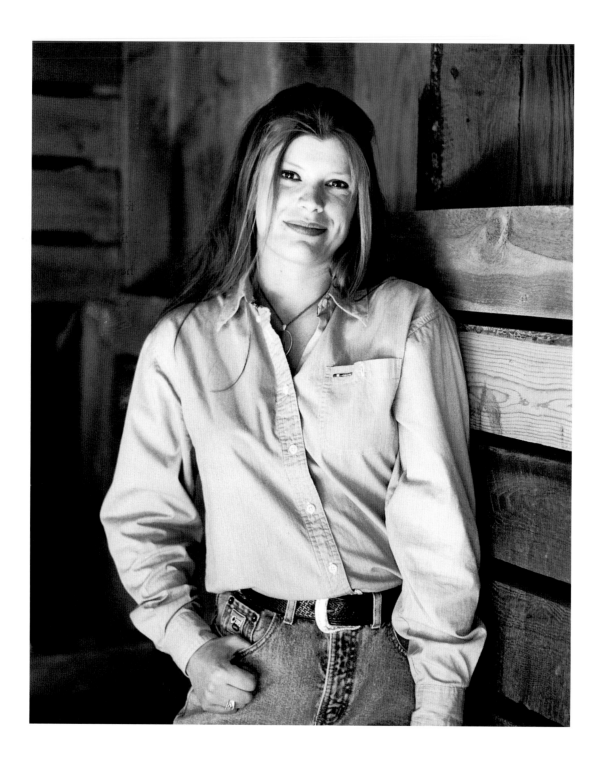

Beau Heath has always wanted to be a champion rodeo barrel racer, but it's been a rough ride so far, mostly because of her hard-luck history with horses. And this Livingston native has logged more than her share of history for someone in her early twenties. She grew up with the rodeo. Her father was a team roper, but it was Aunt Peggy, the only woman in the county who team roped, who was Beau's biggest influence, exposing her to barrel racing when Beau was only four years old. Growing up with horses is not unusual in Montana, but that's about all that's typical in Beau's background. Her grandfather was a Green Beret and a member of the CIA, her mother is French, and one of her neighbors and a good friend is an Iranian princess. What's more, Beau was born partially deaf. "Audiologists say I have only 50 percent hearing, but it seems better than that because I work so hard at it." Because she's an expert lip-reader, you

have no inkling of her hearing impairment until she tells you. And she doesn't let it get in the way of her second love, training horses.

"People ask me why I do it, working with horses, that is. They tell me, 'You have no luck and you're always broke,'" she says as she saddles up

HORSE TRAINER

BEAU HEATH, LIVINGSTON

Flash, a handsome buckskin, her latest pupil. "And it's hard to argue with them. My first horse bled to death after cutting itself on wire. No one discovered it until it was too late." As she checks the cinch, she continues,

"In my junior year in high school, I was so determined to win, but my horse came up lame. That threw me into a slump and I only roped for a few years." She gently pats Flash and talks softly into his ear. To keep oats in his feed bin, she's a waitperson and a clerk at a local western wear store but mostly earns her living by training and breaking horses.

"Rodeo is expensive," Beau laments. A good horse runs $20,000 to $60,000, although the most she ever paid was $4,500, proving you only get what you pay for. "He turned out to be a real basket case. It was a lot to pay for a fifteen-year-old barrel horse," she notes, but she worked hard with the animal until it was ready for the rodeo. However, in true Beau luck, while she was packing her gear for the trip, the horse kicked her brother's horse and ruined its leg—no rodeos that day, or all that summer. Beau forked over more cash for a skin graft for the leg, but during surgery the horse bumped its head and became paralyzed. She worked with it again and this time made it to the rodeo, but she wasn't satisfied with its performance, so she traded it.

Beau is as driven as a barrel horse. She rode and broke colts in high school, but realizing that her riding experience could take her only so far, she attended college in Powell, Wyoming, before transferring to Montana State University to work on an associate of science degree in equine studies. She'd like a bachelor's degree, but MSU won't accept her Powell courses and she'd have to start all over. So for now she's concentrating on establishing a clientele, most notably Tiara, the great-granddaughter of Secretariat. "More and more people are sending their horses to me for barrel training," she says modestly as she pulls a lock of mane out from under Flash's bridle, fussing over him affectionately. If necessary, she'll spend up to a year working with a horse to get it ready for the rodeo. Today her focus is on the buckskin, who was badly beaten by a previous owner and needs to be ridden daily or "you have to retrain him."

Beau works her magic indoors at the Wineglass Arena on a ranch near the entrance to Paradise Valley. Although barrel racing is fast-paced, watching her at work is no spectator sport. Training is slow and deliberate; the important thing is the approach. Control of the horse is 95 percent physical, and Beau puts Flash through his paces, using her legs and the reins rather than her voice. Even though there are three active trainers and horses in the arena, it's surprisingly quiet: These folks break, not beat, their horses. Beau knows the finer points of barrel racing, and the word has spread. Her clients gladly pay a minimum $400 a month for her training skills and pure horse sense, a bargain to those in the know. She also gives riding lessons to kids in her spare time and loves it.

Hearing and equilibrium are closely connected, but to Beau it's not an issue. She says, "You need to have complete balance when you train a horse, and it's actually more difficult when you go slow. It's easy for the horse to sense a rider's shift, which can sometimes throw it off balance slightly." Beau is more than just a pretty face riding a good-looking horse—she's a real working cowgirl who's been thrown, bitten, and stepped on and has the back problems to show for it. But this former Miss Livingston Roundup Rodeo queen is still determined to make it in the horse world.

Not satisfied with several high school rodeo championships, Beau has set her sights on making a living by training and doing rodeos, and she's already halfway there. Her aim is to qualify in barrels for the Wrangler National Finals Rodeo, the best of them all, the one she really wants. Her confidence is contagious, and it's easy to believe her when she says, "I'm gonna get there." ◆

The Bitterroot Valley is timber country with a definite Northwest feel: Its mountainous narrow valleys and timbered hillsides tell you you're not in Ekalaka anymore. Death-defying Route 93 is punctuated by one log-home manufacturer after another. Just north of Hamilton stand two tall monuments that at first glance appear to be really big lawn ornaments but hint at what's inside the spacious new building nearby—George Gulli's workshop. This is one timber buyer who has big plans for his logs: totem poles. Look closer and it becomes profoundly clear that this is not your neighbor's chainsaw-carved bear but rather a lost art, one passed from father to son over more than forty years.

Even before you've taken in the fragrant wood scents or admired his work, George emphatically states that totems are not religious symbols—"that's a myth"—they're status symbols. The taller the totem, the wealthier the family. He explains

Totem Carver

George Gulli, Hamilton

that there are five classes of poles: memorial, mortuary, potlatch (special ceremony), ridicule, and heraldic phratry (similar to a family crest). The major phratries are the thunderbird, raven, bear, eagle, killer whale, and wolf, which varies from tribe to tribe. Colors are regional; for example, the Pacific Northwest and Alaskan tribes favor black, rust red, and ocher, made from natural elements like charcoal and clay.

"Once you know these basics, you can begin to appreciate just about any totem pole," George says.

Carving runs in George's family, beginning with his grandfather, who was a stone carver in Italy, then to his father, and on to George. "Dad was working in a trucking yard in California when he carved his first pole on a tree that had fallen down. He heard about the Marriott theme park that was opening and applied for a job as a wood carver." He wound up making their poles—all fifty-eight of them. A tribal chief saw his work and pronounced it as very well represented, and George's dad was off and running. He became one of the privileged Caucasians sanctioned to carve totems.

Ever the generous man, the senior Gulli "gave" his talent to his son, but it wasn't until George left behind a trail of odd jobs—cannery, welding, construction—that he joined Dad in the business. "I realized I was always happiest when I was carving," he says. Passersby would often see the two of them working outside even in rain and snow, but in severe weather they were limited to carving smaller poles in their tiny outbuilding. When his father died, George picked up where Dad left off, but he's taken totem carving to a higher level. "My poles are art, more than craft, and are more detailed," and although that adds to the cost, there's a two-year waiting list. Like a true artist, George is reluctant to talk about time and money but does say that the more complex a piece is, the more it will cost. "I never thought much about pricing until customers told me I wasn't charging enough—that was a real eye-opener."

George loves the creativity of carving but admits he doesn't enjoy painting the totems and leaves that to his wife, Vonnie. To prevent weathering and fading, he uses a special pole oil to retain their brilliance. Although Native Americans feel there is a limited life span to a pole and it will return to the ground whence it came, George says they could actually last hundreds of years.

The creative process is much more than a weekend project of cutting down a tree, taking a sharp instrument to it, and attaching a price tag—it takes George about four months to carve a typical pole, longer if it's larger or more complex. Like his father, he strives for accuracy but also inserts his own interpretation. He has to figure out the proportions, ratios, shrinkage, and quirks of the wood—each pole gets a new pattern. A template is drawn up and transferred to the log, then a chainsaw quickly removes the waste parts—again, he stresses "*not* the same as chainsaw art," which he adds is often not even sawed by hand anymore but mass-produced. Now George's heritage kicks in—

he sands and files until he's satisfied. Only then is it ready for the Gulli signature.

In his studio are three poles in various stages of development: a smaller one has been carved and is waiting for a thunderbird's wings, a larger pole has been roughed out, and a third has the pattern drawn on. George uses mostly larch for its beauty and durability as well as the way it checks (the way wood cracks when it dries), and although spruce and cottonwood are nice to work with, "they check like an open book," so he avoids them. These days he rarely sets foot in the forest in search of the perfect pole, relying instead on referrals and rejects from log-home manufacturers or sawmills.

Although his wood is local, his customers certainly aren't. Consider the man from Utah who gladly shelled out thousands for three big totems and is back on the waiting list for another. On the flip side is the guy who paid for his pole but never claimed it despite George's repeated calls and letters for five years and counting.

Like a proud parent with hundreds of photos of his kids, George flips through an album chock-full of his work: totems as residential and commercial outdoor decorations, as indoor structural items, and of course more than a few on reservations, the last a testament to his skills. He's even been asked by Native Americans to show them how to carve, but his skill "is something that can't easily be taught."

Not all totems are the same. George's Web site (www.geocities.com/gullitotems) explains that a genuine pole is sanctioned, and George's are. As one of the few non–Native Americans in the country given the nod by the Northwest Pacific Coast tribes, his legacy grows—one phratry at a time. ◆

It's Christmas Eve. Santa Claus is getting into his red Dodge pickup and heading home—to Glasgow, Montana. As he's done since 1994, Jim Jensen has put in fourteen-hour days, seven days a week between Thanksgiving and Christmas, and he loves it. His popularity as a shopping mall Santa has grown—along with his beard and girth—ever since he first donned the red velvet suit.

His Santa career began ironically when he was stranded in action in Vietnam. He and his buddies let their beards grow, and although he eventually shaved his off, he kept the mustache. Years later he let his beard grow in as well. Then a friend suggested he apply for work as a Santa. Jim was laid off from his job as an addictions counselor, so he figured, why not? He hired an agent who landed him his first Kris Kringle gig, which was in California, but later decided he could do it better himself. At this point he didn't have enough white hair to be convincing, so he bleached his beard and hair. "I'm now naturally white," he says, stating the obvious.

SANTA BROKER

JIM JENSEN, GLASGOW

Jim loves kids, so playing Santa came easily. Today he provides a complete package that includes helpers, a photographer, and high-end digital photographic equipment to the malls that hire him. But as any adult knows, Santa can't be everywhere at once, so he expanded his business by recruiting other look-alikes to go on location. His Web site (www.jjssantas.com) has photos and biographies of numerous wannabes. Jim has sent Santas out to various malls, from Hong Kong to Pittsburgh. JJ's Santas look the part—all have natural beards and hair and are appropriately portly. Each man is thoroughly screened before being accepted for Santahood. But don't expect them to "Ho-Ho-Ho"—"We don't do it. It often scares the kids. Training is mostly commonsense things, and of course they have to like kids." His jolly old clones range from a retired meatcutter to a seasonal park ranger to one who specializes in e-mail letters from kids.

Things are a little different today, and part of the training includes the all-important caution to keep hands visible at all times—even Santa isn't immune to lawsuits. Equally as important, Jim stresses to "never abuse the power you have over the kids. I'm constantly amazed at how much they believe I'm Santa and totally trust me."

Contrary to popular belief, most youngsters sitting on Santa's knee don't pull on his whiskers. "They don't want to make the old guy mad at Christmastime," he chuckles. "It's the parents who tell the kids to tug on my beard. Once I had it yanked only because a grandmother insisted. But I really wish they wouldn't. When I hear Mom or Dad suggest it, I want to add that I wouldn't mind if you told the children not to stick their fingers in my eyes, either."

Another myth is that kids rattle off their wish list as soon as they land on Jim's well-padded lap. Not so. Many are there for the photo op and nothing more. But that's not to say the kids don't want anything; in fact, Jim notices that the requests have become more self-centered—nuts to little brother or even Mom and Dad.

In spite of nearly seven thousand kids who climb onto his lap each season, he's had only two leaky diapers and one girl "who hated my guts. She came every Christmas for about seven years, then finally gave me a big hug." Not all stories have such a happy ending. He doesn't hesitate when asked about his worst moment. It was bittersweet. "I noticed a small boy and his mother, who was holding a baby, standing in line. It was clear the mother had been crying. I love babies. I've held lots of them and thought something didn't look quite right with this one. The mother handed me the infant and said, 'Give my baby wings.' The child was dying. We all just stopped and cried for a while."

And then there are the memories that make him smile. He recalls one child who said, "I love you more better than my mommy," which makes one wonder what this kid's home life was like. And he gets a kick out of what he refers to as the "four-foot wall." It's the space in front of him that transforms eager two-year-olds into panic-stricken screamers. He cautions parents about it, yet most ignore him and frequently leave with teary-eyed tots in tow.

He's recognized as Santa all year, even after he trims back his beard. "One summer while I was walking through the mall, a little girl recognized me and waved timidly. I winked back at her." It's this unspoken communication with kids that Jim really enjoys. Another time he was approached by a small boy who boldly said, "You look like Santa." Jim replied smiling, "How do you know I'm not?" The boy thought for a moment, then taking no chances, replied, "Do you want a piece of candy?"

That one still makes Jim laugh out loud. Even adults don't want to tempt fate. Once without proper identification and nothing more than his checkbook in hand, Jim was able to buy a rock concert ticket when the manager intervened, saying, "He's Santa. His check's good."

In the off-season Jim stays plenty busy. He runs a small photo studio in his home, he and his wife operate a concession stand at powwows selling shaved ice, and he still works as an addictions counselor on a consulting basis. Even though it means leaving his wife behind for five weeks, come Thanksgiving he goes to the mall like everyone else. In his case it's because he looks forward to meeting the thousands of kids who are waiting for him to make their Christmas official. He says, "I love this job." What more could anyone ask for? ◆

In a world where bigger is considered better, Orvin Fjare will most likely disagree with you. He creates miniatures. It all started with a groundhog, sort of. For sixty years he hadn't bought his wife, Sigrid, an anniversary or birthday present, instead giving her a bottle of perfume every Groundhog Day. But after forty bottles she announced she'd always wanted a dollhouse, so Orvin grabbed up his tools and went to work. From a *Billings Gazette* clipping he copied an architect's drawings and began construction. The result was more than Sigrid bargained for: a modern 1960s dollhouse complete with a miniature photo of the couple on the bedroom dresser; plus a re-creation of *Gone with the Wind's* Tara, featuring sweeping staircases with Scarlet poised to descend; and a Norwegian log home with handcrafted mousetrap and outhouse.

That was the easy part. Now Orvin needed furniture but couldn't find what he

MINIATURES MAKER

ORVIN FJARE, BIG TIMBER

wanted, so he decided to make his own. This decision was not untypical for Orvin. He always liked woodworking; in fact, one day years ago he told Sigrid he was going to make a living room set, which is still in use. As a boy of twelve, he made a small wooden pistol with a revolving barrel, but he never really had an interest in miniatures until he started making the dollhouses.

There's nothing in Orvin's background that hints at his passion for Lilliputia. After serving as a doughboy in World War I, he worked with his father-in-law in the family clothing business, which he figured he'd do the rest of his life. But one thing led to another, and his knack for public affairs landed him in government. He started as a U.S. congressman in 1955 and was eventually appointed by Richard Nixon to the Federal Housing Administration in Helena, with stints in the state legislature and as director of the Montana Department of Tourism in between.

He retired at the age of sixty-nine and turned to miniatures full-time.

The Big Timber resident made his first piece of tiny furniture in 1985. Three years later, out of curiosity, Orvin and Sigrid attended a miniatures show in Spokane—he was hooked. That same year he sold his first creation, prompting him to go to another show, this time as a seller. He displayed one of his fully furnished dollhouses, and the Fjare reputation began. Soon he was selling at up to fourteen shows a year and doing very well: From Philly to Chicago to Anaheim, avid collectors looked for his work. And let's make it clear—this is not your average Popsicle stick and Elmer's glue stuff. He has elevated his miniatures to a fine art, specializing in elaborate Victorian pieces that fetch prices to match. Each piece is signed and numbered, not the kind of stuff you let the kids bang around. Dedicated collectors, who spend as much as $30,000 to outfit a full house, barely blink at dropping $595 for one of Orvin's grandfather clocks.

It wasn't long before their breakfast nook became his workroom. Jammed into the 10-by-9-foot area is every imaginable power and hand tool, only smaller. The room is a miniature furniture factory: Stacks of various woods, knobs, pulls, dowels, and assorted doodads are everywhere. Orvin notes his "state-of-the-art" bookkeeping system, pointing to handwritten orders taped to the windows in front of his workbench.

For a man who admittedly has no patience, his work is remarkably detailed. On a scale of 1 inch equaling 1 foot, drawers open, castors on the swivel chair turn, even the grandfather clock keeps time. His rolltop desk is made of individual ⅛-inch-wide slats (the size of toothpicks) glued to a linen hankie, and like every piece he makes, it functions. He says no self-respecting rolltop would be without a secret compartment and opens a drawer to reveal another, hidden drawer with a bottle of whiskey—empty, he points out. The walnut desk took him forty to fifty hours to make—cost for both is $695, chair alone is $95.

Factoring in materials and marketing, that translates to barely better than minimum wage.

According to his brochure, the "hallmark of Fjare miniatures" is the Wooten cabinet secretary, the Swiss Army knife of furniture. He makes two grades: The Superior sells for $1,900; the Extra-grade at $1,200 a pop is his best seller. They each feature brass hardware and nearly one hundred drawers so tiny you almost need tweezers to open them. At shows his musical player piano, as well as other pieces, sell themselves because would-be buyers can handle them—the only major breakage was his own fault, he says.

Everything he makes is from a photo, using no patterns except for the ones he draws himself. His talent has not gone unnoticed: He's been featured in several miniatures magazines and was the cover story in one of them. And he gets mail—letters of thanks and praise such as the one from a woman who was so thrilled with her Wooten desk that to avoid squabbles, she ordered two more so she could leave one to each of her children in her will. But one letter stands out. Orvin plucks a faded note from the workshop wall. A woman returned her Superior Wooten because he had numbered it 13. Apparently suffering from triskaidekaphobia, she was offended that he'd send her such an atrocity. So, Orvin did the only sensible thing: He changed the number to 18 and sent the desk to someone else, who was thrilled with it.

Orvin has a mind full of ideas but admits that the travel to shows is a hassle, so he sells only by mail and custom orders. "I want to taper off. I need all the fun I can get—I have enough orders to keep me busy for a year." It won't cost you big bucks to see Orvin's handiwork. At Big Timber's Crazy Mountain Museum, there's a scale model of the town circa 1900, buildings by Orvin. And to think he owes this all to a groundhog. ✦

Between Harrison and Norris at the base of the Tobacco Root Mountains lies the Sitz ranch, a calendar-pretty spot. In this remote part of the state, Sitz cows greatly outnumber the towns' residents, yet this ranch is known internationally for its quality of breeding cattle. Twice a year cows become the minority as hundreds of cattle buyers descend on the ranch to place bids on Sitz Angus bulls.

"People want to buy from reputable breeders," says Bob Sitz. And these are the best. They're products of more than seventy-five years of disciplined cattle breeding that began with Bob's grandparents in Nebraska, where his grandmother bought their first registered seed cattle. Dad moved to Montana in 1960 and quickly established the Sitz name as premier among cattlemen. The ranch's twenty-three thousand acres are spread between Bob and his brother, Jim, who manages the Dillon herd. His sisters also raise cattle, in South Dakota and

CONSERVATION RANCHER

BOB SITZ, HARRISON

New Zealand, but Harrison is the heart of the operation. Bob says that to get the proper experience, "all us kids had to work on a different ranch out of high school before coming back home to work." When his father died in a tractor accident, Bob and Jim were prepared to take over, "but my mother is still the ranch's strength."

When you sell a bull for the price of a brand-new fully loaded pickup, you'd better know what you're doing, and Bob does. What he hadn't learned from his father he picked up in agricultural business courses at Montana State University, loading up on classes in genetics and range management. This education was instrumental in giving the ranch its reputation as a conservation benchmark as well as a cattle operation.

When his parents bought the property, there was no functioning water supply, the fields needed reseeding, and the buildings were run-down, hardly today's neatly manicured grounds with barely a pebble out of place. The first thing they did was to fix the irrigation canal, then install a gravity-fed system that irrigates twenty-four hundred acres efficiently, saving on precious water. Once electricity was run to the range and forest-land, two pumps and 35 miles of pipe were added to supply forty stock tanks, which are shared by elk, deer, moose, bear—nearly every type of Montana's fauna.

Bob didn't set out to become a conservation rancher; he just wanted to improve his herd, and what's good for cows is usually good for wildlife. "I read a report that compared all different kinds of wildlife to cattle; for example, the impact of five deer or 260 gophers is the same as having another cow. So I figure when it comes to crop consumption, the ranch's wildlife equals four hundred more head." When he added ponds and improved streamsides, it wasn't only cattle that started living the good life. He takes the property's carrying capacity into consideration to make sure the land can support everything. This means prac-

ticing "rest rotation," in which each year one of their four forest pastures goes unused.

Water is always an issue, especially in the West—battles have been fought over it. To maintain a healthy supply, the ranch has five lakes, stocked with brookies and rainbows. He fenced off some streams and planted trees to help improve riparian areas. Cattle are kept out of certain streams and lakes, preventing overgrazed shorelines and ensuring clean water—management that's allowed him to maximize the land's capacity, thus maintaining the number of cattle. Four settling ponds, "similar to what cities do," were built to purify runoff from their feedlot. Bob improved several major spawning areas, including a large dredge pit left over from eighty years of mining. Water attracts ducks and geese as well as sandhill cranes and great blue herons. Controlled burns and weed management provide habitat for upland game birds. Bald and golden eagles, swans, bluebirds, foxes, coyotes, and many more critters make the ranch a virtual refuge.

The conservation efforts of the Sitzes haven't gone unnoticed. Office walls are adorned with plaques and awards, "in recognition of natural resource stewardship practices, which contribute to the environment and enhance productivity and profitability," according to one. The Montana Stock-growers Association was so impressed that it nominated the Sitz ranch for the state environmental stewardship award, which led to its winning at the U.S. regional level. The 1991 National Angus Journal Land Stewardship Award was the Sitzes', too. These honors were bestowed not only by peer groups such as the National Cattlemen's Association but also the Nature Conservancy, among others.

It all pays off the first Thursday each December, when the machinery barn is converted into a sale arena lined with bleachers that fill quickly. In a fast-paced four hours, one bull is sold every thirty seconds. This sale combined with the smaller one in Dillon accounts for 95 percent of the ranch's income; the majority of the sales are to repeat buyers, who show up from throughout the world.

Sitz auctions are practically a community event, where Harrison high school students help out to earn money for their class trip. And although the complimentary lunch alone is worth the trip, it's more likely that bidders are here for some of the best seed stock on the planet. Bulls and heifers alike take the stage before the gavel hits.

"People come to buy from us because they like our program, reputation, and service," Bob says. And to make sure it stays that way, the ranch employs ten people who help do AI (artificial insemination)—their busiest time—breeding studies, and constant testing to ensure good stock. "Buyers know that because our females are bred at higher elevations, the performance and longevity are built in."

If you're in the market for a breeding bull or just curious about how a ranch should be run, get on the list for a Sitz ranch Angus or wildlife tour (www.sitzangus.com). You'll see that although the way he does things has cost Bob extra time and money, the rewards are well worth it. ◆

For years Jack Schwend hung on to the dusty old fiddle handed down by his grandfather. It wasn't until he retired from ranching, however, that he had the time to look at it closely. The fiddle came to Bridger, Montana, with his grandfather in 1888, so Jack figures it is at least that old. He thinks it was made in the South because that's where his grandfather was raised. It has no markings but is constructed of a southern wood, another clue to its origin, but that's about all he knows. With plenty of free time, he decided to dust off the instrument, have it repaired, and figure out how to play it.

At age sixty-five, with fiddle in hand, he found a teacher in Miles City who gave him the basics in a few lessons; from there Jack took off on his own. You'll never see him playing at Carnegie Hall, but he has polished his skills enough that he can teach others. His interest didn't stop with playing and teaching however; he was fascinated with the fiddle's construction. Upon seeing a magazine article for ordering a fiddle pattern, Jack sent in the required $16 and soon began making his own. It wasn't long before a sign the size of a license plate appeared on his bunkhouse that reads JACK'S MUSIC SHOP—definitely a low-key operation.

FIDDLE MAKER

JACK SCHWEND, ROSEBUD

Inside the shop the wall is lined with about a dozen fiddles and mandolins. There's even the rare mandoviol, which is actually Jack's own concoction, a hybrid of sorts of a mandolin head on a fiddle body. He says, "It has a different feel for playing, and the sound is unique." The instruments are a rainbow of natural and dyed woods, lacquered and polished to a high gloss. Two wine-red mandolins stand out from the rest, but the real eye-catcher sits on the counter. It has strange red lines and numbers running vertically and the words *Hardware Hank* sprinkled about. This mandolin is made of wooden yardsticks, not entirely unusual for Jack—most of his instruments are made of found woods.

Jack says that although fiddles are usually made of maple with spruce fronts, his instruments break from tradition because he gets his materials where he can. A familiar face at the local landfill, he once found an old piano whose leg is now a fiddle neck. Another neck and fingerboard are courtesy of an ax handle, and one mandolin's body is fashioned from the board of an old truck bed. When the Catholic church in Rosebud discarded its pews, Jack had visions of mandolin bodies and happily hauled them home. But easily the conversation pieces are the two mandolins that sport *Ace Hardware* and *Hardware Hank*.

There's a distinctive smell, not unpleasant, of varnish and stain that tells you this is a working shop. Jack is always looking for woods that will give his music makers an interesting grain, and he is proud of the one he made of Russian olive, a "trash tree" that has surprisingly beautiful graining. For the bodies he starts with a plank that's nearly an inch thick, which he carves and sands to create the bowed look. It's a good thing he's retired, because each masterpiece takes a couple months to complete; however, he usually has more than one in the works. And like the great masters, he signs and dates each one.

Jack's Music Shop is not a for-profit business by any means—he has sold only one instrument since he hung out his shingle. But others *have* profited through his donations as fund-raisers, such as the girls from Rosebud who needed money for a European music tour. He donated a mandolin, which they raffled for $1,200. And Rosebud High School has football once again, thanks in part to Jack. Looking to field a team after a twenty-year absence, the school needed to raise money. Among the items donated for auction was one of his mandolins, which fetched a healthy $750; another donation to the Custer High School FFA brought $150. And there will be others.

Jack is a self-taught musician, yet since the mid-1990s he's helped at least twenty others to play. "I can get them started, but most of them now would make me look sick." He guarantees to have anyone playing a tune in half an hour or less. In his shop today, his student struggles just to hold the instrument, much less create anything resembling music. In fact, she's absolutely awful, but Jack has enormous patience and urges her to continue her attempt at "Bile Them Cabbage Down." He never charges for lessons, but this session could change all that. The student's husband rolls his eyes and suggests she stick to writing.

Jack's a real pick-up-and-play musician who doesn't follow printed music: "I can read somewhat but it takes me all day to figure it out." This approach fits in just fine with his pals at the Eastern Montana Old Time Fiddlers in Miles City, half an hour away. Since 1994 he's happily jammed with this independent group.

So what could be better? For Jack it's a music hall closer to home in downtown Rosebud.

That was his plan when he bought the old Odd Fellows building. At 18 by 60 feet, it's like a huge boxcar that's sparse on amenities. When asked if it has central heating, Jack chuckles, "Well, the woodstove is in the middle of the room." He brought the electric up to code, installed a small stage at one end, and added benches that provide seating for about 50. Now on Sunday afternoons Rosebud rocks when musicians and aficionados gather to immerse themselves in the sounds of old-time country music.

If you've been through Rosebud, you'll notice that it's not exactly the heart of Montana's timber industry. More than once Jack has had to negotiate stacks of wood left at his doorstep by those interested in contributing to the arts. But Jack's not complaining—he's always looking for the fiddle in the rough. ◆

Mary Harker thinks about Christmas 365 days a year. Sometimes it's as pastor of the United Methodist Church, where twenty people on a Sunday is a good crowd, but mostly it's when tending to her congregation of Christmas trees that she raises in Heron. Tucked into the wilderness of northwest Montana, her 100-acre spread is so close to the state line that if she were any farther west, she'd be raising potatoes.

Christmas trees were the last thing on Mary's mind when she met her late husband. "We were both going to school in Missoula. He was the only fellow on campus who could walk faster than me," she jokes. John had always wanted to raise and sell trees when he retired, but when the bottom fell out of their dairy business, he began planting. "We had a bad hay season and that did us in," says Mary.

Cedar Farm—in Montana's banana belt—gets 34 inches of rain a year, so trees seemed more practical and profitable than cows, but they soon found there's more to growing trees than sticking seedlings in the ground, sitting back, and watching them mature. "The first year we planted ten acres, but they died." The second year they replanted, this time with Douglas fir; they died, too. The third year—again no luck. Finally, the fourth year they planted grand fir on a different part of the property—they thrived. "It seems the original spot had too much clay and got too damp."

It takes ten years for a tree to reach 8 feet, the best size for selling, so they realized they needed help and eagerly joined the Inland Empire Christmas Tree Growers Association. Mary speaks very highly of the group: Through it she learned how to run the business and John got an education in raising trees.

To say that tree farming is labor intensive is an understatement, so as head of the operation, Mary now leaves the physical work to her son. The

CHRISTMAS TREE GROWER

MARY HARKER, HERON

perfect tree starts with prepping the ground in fall so two-year-old seedlings can be planted in spring. As they grow they need to be shaped by shearing, a process Mary has avoided. "Sometimes you can know too much. Don't learn to milk cows and don't learn how to shear trees. If you don't know how, you won't have to do it, and it's no fun." It's hard, hot, sticky work, fending off mosquitoes and yellow jackets while wielding a machete. Pruning is done before trees break bud in spring, then continues once the new growth hardens, something she learned in a class offered by the association. But trees need to be shaped or every one will be unattractive—a "Charlie Brown"—so these days they hire someone to do it. After cutting, old stumps need to be removed to make room for new plants—still more hard work.

Like any farmer, Mary has to deal with crop pests but hers are the size of elk; actually they *are* elk. She points to section B-10 and notes, "They eat the Fraser firs like ice cream. One year thirteen head and their calves played Fox and Geese around the trees and had trails going all over the place in the snow," trampling some of the smaller trees.

In summer pocket gophers pick up where ruminants leave off, nibbling at young roots. Meanwhile knapweed and orange hawkweed spread out and take over the ground, sucking up precious water. Although Heron is one of the state's wetter spots, Mary still has to deal with weather. Once they lost two years of planting because it was too dry and only one hundred trees made it out the twelve thousand they planted. "Most winters there's not too much snow but in some, like in 1996, there was so much we had to plow the fields to finish the harvest." And fire is a four-letter word any time of year.

Despite all the setbacks, come November Mary has trees to sell. Most are sold wholesale and trucked from New Jersey to California. "One reseller in Lewistown brought a bunch of church kids who did all the cutting and loading. I think they financed a trip to Israel with the proceeds."

Each year groups like the Lions Club in Libby and the Boy Scouts in St. Regis come to Mary for trees to sell as fund-raisers.

Although surrounded by thousands of acres of forest, about one hundred people each season prefer to "choose and cut" one of Mary's trees than schlep through the woods in search of their own. Single-tree buyers have shown up at Cedar Farm as late as Christmas Eve, but instead of Mary they do business with the honor box, her silent partner.

The perfect tree is in the eye of the buyer; and although nicely shaped ones sell best, some people come looking specifically for a Charlie Brown tree. "One person wanted a tree that was bare on one side so they could put it against a wall.

I've even seen one painted black," she says. Most folks snap up grand firs, but Mary's favorite is the cork bark (like a soft-needled fir), which she thinks looks the most natural. It's considered good luck to find a bird's nest in your Christmas tree but Mary doesn't charge extra if you do. "There's one price, whether it's wholesale or retail—it takes the same amount of work to raise a tree for a wholesaler as anybody else."

Mary sees fewer competitors each year. "The market is still there so I expect more people to get into the tree growing business." Although there have been a few years of decline, she thinks it will come back. But she really can't dwell on it; the concolor firs in section A-2 need pruning. ✦

John Phillips is a name-dropper—George Armstrong Custer, Henry Plummer, William Rogers Clark, Sacajawea—he knows them all and knows them well. John is a Montana history expert, a hands-on historian who's more familiar with Captain Clark than Clark's own mother. In fact, a favorite part of his job is to dress up as the great explorer for interpretive tours at Pompeys Pillar, site of the only remaining physical proof of the Lewis and Clark expedition.

John is passionate about Lewis and Clark, but he wasn't always that way. Like many history majors, he did anything but historical work after graduating from college. Before he went on to graduate school, he put in his time at a liquor store and behind an office desk before he was accepted at the University of Montana, where he focused on western history. His internship at Bannack State Park was responsible for his thesis

LEWIS AND CLARK INTERPRETIVE GUIDE

JOHN PHILLIPS, POMPEYS PILLAR

on vigilantes and his deepening interest in Montana history. But it wasn't until the Bureau of Land Management hired him to work at Pompeys Pillar that John found his niche in history. "I never had a good-paying job, but I work in what I love. The pillar is perfect—outside, casual, and unlike most government seasonal jobs, I get to interact with people." Here John drops a few more names, this time a couple of contemporary ones. "I met the noted author-historian Steven Ambrose but was off the day Conan O'Brien came through—surprisingly he's a history buff, too." It's the opportunity to interact with visiting historians that makes his job a learning experience for him as well, a nice perk, according to John.

Unlike interpretive lecturers at most historical sites, John more than immerses himself in his work. Whether for scout or school groups, Audubon field trips, or the casual tourist, once or twice a week he dons his buckskin suit and for about thirty minutes becomes Captain Clark, speaking in the first person and taking the listener back roughly two hundred years. John says some people question his long auburn ponytail as being historically correct, but he says, "We think it's accurate and fits in with the period. Clark was military, he had to enlist, but although there were no regulations about hair length, there were for bathing," and rest assured John does bathe. The ponytail was most likely sported by Clark, who was known as the Red-Headed Chief. Not only is John's physical resemblance to Clark uncanny, but the fact that he was born in the same Missouri town where Clark is buried raises a few eyebrows in his audience.

John's conversations are peppered with historical trivia. He relates details that you won't find in any brochure or history book and makes it sound as though it all happened just last week. He says, "Clark was actually a lieutenant, not a captain, but his men were not told any different. He wasn't given that rank until 2001." Here and there another nuttle pops out: "At one point there was a huge fight in Congress on whether to name our state Abyssinia or Copperhead. . . . On his way to the Little Bighorn Colonel Gibbon described the condition of Clark's signature on the pillar, making me wonder about the history of the signature itself. . . . The pronunciation and spelling of *Sacajawea* are still in dispute; even Lewis and Clark had trouble pronouncing it and called her Janey instead; never so much controversy over a name. . . . Clark is credited for discovering only one thing on the Yellowstone River, a sucker fish. . . ." And so it goes.

Since the early 1990s John has entertained visitors to the pillar, but that's only part of his job. Along with the more common task of mowing the lawn, he catches rattlesnakes, which he releases on other less-visited public lands. He also mentions the harmless resident bull snakes and was amused by the Girl Scout group that happened to be there while the snakes were mating, a rather violent ritual. "I told them the snakes are mating, and you can ask your leader about that," he chuckles. (If you want to see this spectacle yourself, late April or early May is best.) One of the more serious events at the pillar involved a dog that was swept away by the river but much to the owner's relief was rescued three days later by a fisherman who noticed the dog's red harness. John helped reunite owner with pet. Worse was the day when an elderly man from Minnesota collapsed from a heart attack while hiking to the top of the pillar. As John helped administer CPR, a medevac was summoned—"the only time a chopper landed up there," he notes.

If you visit Pompeys Pillar in the off-season, John won't be there. On what has become an annual trek between November and April when he's not earning extra income building fences, he hits the road to visit friends and relatives and scours historic sites in Canada, New Mexico, and Utah. A favorite stop each year is Zion National Park where, in Corps of Discovery style, he camps whenever he can, then "loops back" through Wisconsin before reaching Montana.

As sure as the coming of spring, however, is John's return to the pillar. He'll be there for the annual event known as Clark's Day to relive that moment in July 1806 when Clark and eight others floated down this stretch of the Yellowstone. Because of the excellent journals the men kept, we even know the exact time they brought their boats ashore: 4:00 P.M.

Captain Clark's stop at the pillar is only one part of the rock's history. John likes to relate historical events to each other and notes that the pillar was an important site for many types of people—frontiersmen, cavalry, Native Americans, railroaders, and trappers, among others. But when you listen to John talk about it, you'll understand why it holds a special importance for him. ◆

It's an uncharacteristically damp and dreary Montana summer morning. The Bozeman farmers' market, which is usually bustling, is a bit slower today, but the crowd is drawn to a specific booth. They're standing five deep to see what vegetables the vendor dressed in white shirt, suspenders, and straw hat will lay out next. A tourist might question this unusual fascination with produce, but the locals know better—this is special; this is Hutterite stuff. Sam Hofer's appearance is as distinctive as his produce. With his neatly trimmed beard and wire-frame glasses, he enjoys near celebrity status from his regular customers. He and another similarly dressed man have made the 78-mile trip from the Springdale colony as they do every Saturday in the summer.

Although there are twenty-five such colonies throughout Montana, the Hutterites remain a mystery to many, which has led to lots of

HUTTERITE ELDER

SAM HOFER,
WHITE SULPHUR SPRINGS

misinformation. Sam is quick to clarify: "We're not a cult, we're a religious group, a sect." It's a Christ-based religion that differs from other Christian faiths in its strict interpretation of a New Testament passage that says true believers should be together and share all their possessions. In the 1500s Jacob Hutter became the leader of this breakaway pacifist group and ironically was burned at the stake while his followers were imprisoned. During their incarceration they wrote the sermons that Sam says have been passed down for generations and are still used today.

Sam's colony sits just west of White Sulphur Springs, its quiet location befitting its lifestyle. But it's a working colony—a hardworking colony—and everyone has duties in this highly structured and industrious community. Each member wears many hats. Sam, for example, is schoolteacher, member of the board of directors, produce seller, husband, and father to five daughters and four sons. It's difficult if not impossible to single out one member from the rest because they are all so integrated. When asked about himself, Sam automatically tells you about the colony. Like each member, Sam is the colony and representative of it.

The living quarters comprise just a few acres of their land. At 140 people it's a large group, almost outgrowing its capacity, but Sam says, "We find it hard to branch off because land is so expensive." With so many people there needs to be harmony. Everyone gets along because it's pretty hard to avoid someone you see every day.

What's more, the Hutterite colony is a business. To maintain a community this size, they need to generate a lot of income for equipment, building materials, health care, and occasionally some outside expertise. Although they're known for their organically grown produce, it's hardly the main source of revenue. Their primary enterprise is producing milk and raising pork, sheep, and beef to sell to major meat processors. And Hutterite chickens are often highlighted on menus in finer restau-

rants throughout the state. "People think because we're a religious group, we don't pay taxes, but they're wrong—we sure do, and plenty of them," Sam says. He's very proud of his colony, which has a reputation for its good people and its strong relationship with nearby towns. "We try to do most of our business locally," assures Sam, but admits that to save money they'll sometimes buy in bulk at warehouse stores.

Everyone here is provided for, but instead of salaries, they are given allowances. When young married couples set up housekeeping, they receive everything they need, including a sewing machine to make the signature plaid dresses and polka-dot head scarves that the girls are seldom without at home and never without in public. Clothes are dark because it's more humble and they wear no jewelry—not even wedding bands, although married men do sport beards. In many ways it's a very utopian life. As a result, the Hutterites have been approached by outsiders who want to join the religion, but it won't happen—you must be born into it. It's not for everyone, though; even though their fifteen thousand chickens enjoy state-of-the-art computerized housing, there's not a radio or television on the premises, and to leave the colony for even a few hours you must get permission from its governing board of directors. Sam says, "Since we moved here in 1958, several teenage boys have [permanently] left the colony, but most have returned."

Sam's colony is the *Lehre* (German for "teacher"), the most conservative of the religion's three sects. For twenty-two years he has taught German as the main language, and singing, but it's all a cappella—musical instruments are not allowed. Education is from kindergarten through ninth grade, after which the young adults get vocational training to become part of the workforce. To meet state education requirements, students are taught by public schoolteachers, something the colony originally footed the bill for, but by merg-

ing with the White Sulphur Springs school district, that cost was covered. The benefit to the school district was having the additional students, which increased the amount of its state funding—a win-win situation.

While sitting in Sam's modern housing unit, we can't help but notice how sparsely it's furnished. There's no kitchen, only a sink, because all meals are taken in the communal dining hall. Little adorns the walls, calling even more attention to the all-important clock. At exactly 3:15 a bell rings, and Sam's daughters, potato peelers in hand, join the other women in the main kitchen, where they spend fifteen minutes peeling the next meal's potatoes. Later, as our interview winds down, Sam checks the clock once more and encourages the girls to sing for us before we leave. Time stops as we listen to pure voices in perfect harmony—in a word, angelic. The bell rings again. Church service is about to begin. ◆

When asked why he decided to become a wildlife biologist, Chuck Jonkel jokes, "I thought being outside would be better than cutting hair." His nonstop conversation is sprinkled with quick wit and sarcasm. He points out that more than one biologist started out as a poacher, and he was no exception. As kids growing up in Wisconsin, Chuck and his brother illegally shot a white-tailed deer, "So I guess you could say we were interested in wildlife."

A decade later, and wiser, he was still pursuing wildlife but this time armed with a handful of degrees, including a PhD. Initially his interest was in geology, "then my brother pointed out that geologists were always digging holes and biologists were filling them up, so I changed my major." Chuck's first wildlife study was pine marten research near Whitefish. In 1959 he got two real job offers—raking leaves on the University of Montana campus or studying

GRIZZLY BEAR EXPERT

CHUCK JONKEL, MISSOULA

bears. "Raking actually paid better, but being a biologist, I figured I should take the bear job." He says he never actually set out to study bears. "They always seemed to find me."

As Chuck was finishing the study, bears found him again when the Canadian government tapped him for polar bear research. Before that was completed, bears tracked him down once more, this time in Montana for research on grizzlies around Glacier National Park. He prefers to work on bears outside the parks, where they exist in a more natural and wild state and are not as heavily studied. "A bear sneezes in Yellowstone and two or three senators have to run out there to see what's going on," he says.

Early on, Chuck became known as "the bear guy," and his reputation spread worldwide. Gradually his interest shifted from field research to education. He knew that making the information entertaining as well as informative would add to its appeal. What followed has become a Missoula mainstay—the International Wildlife Film Festival, which Chuck founded and ran for twenty-four years.

The more Chuck worked with bears, the more he saw how flawed education programs were. "Even some of the literature the government puts out is wrong," he says. "There were things that weren't getting done, and more than once I half joked about having an institute for bear study." Once more the bears came knocking: This time it was two men with a plan. In 1982 bruins everywhere got their own union when the Great Bear Foundation was formed. Its mission is "the conservation of wild bear populations and their habitat worldwide." Chuck laments, "Most of our financing comes from contributions, but like so many nonprofits, since 9/11 money is tight.

"By saving the bears we also protect what they represent—they're symbolic of what is wild about Montana," Chuck states. Nothing gets him riled more than people who exploit bears, like the Grizzly Center in West Yellowstone. Promoting itself as an educational experience, he says it does quite the opposite, misleading visitors about what is natural, real, and safe. Nearly as disconcerting is the topic of removing the grizzly from the endangered species list (delisting). "If it happens, control will fall back onto the state," he says, adding, "I could support delisting if Helena would provide the funds to properly manage bears."

Crucial to bear survival is habitat, which has gotten better, but on private lands it has become smaller. "So, all together in one bucket, habitat has gotten worse," he says. Although the park service and Bureau of Land Management are doing a better job, "sprawl, logging, even fire camps during fire season nickel-and-dime bears to death."

Attitudes have changed. "Now bears are getting more public support. People photograph them, write about them, and spend money just to watch them. Landowners are excited to see them; they don't automatically run for their guns." Hunting, too, has changed—instead of an open season, it's more aesthetic. It took several years of Chuck's hard work, but now in Montana bears are regarded as game animals and require a hunting license. Exempt, of course, is the government, which still has "hired guns" who shoot predators—they were still killing grizzlies three years after they were listed. A basic tenet in nature is that predators are part of the big picture, which is why Chuck feels education is so important.

So all year, he's either teaching courses in the wild or on the road leading field trips, including polar bear classes in Canada. "Three of Montana's rivers empty into Hudson's Bay, so even polar bears hundreds of miles away are affected by what we do here." They're easy to see and not aggressive, "but they're uninhibited, and I sometimes have to hustle people back into the vans." That's not the case in Glacier, where grizzlies and black bears are less inquisitive, more secretive, and harder to find. If one of Chuck's classes at the Glacier Institute has a bearless day, his students don't sit idle—they can look for tracks, rubbings, or other things bears leave in the woods.

"I've had encounters but I've never been attacked." Chuck attributes this fact to his ability to interpret bear body language. What about the rest of us? "Bear bells are okay but really, any kind of noise will do. Hammer a log with a stick—just let them know you're there." In fact, humans seeking bears is a bigger problem. People coax them to their backyards with birdseed and dog food, and that's a tough habit to break—and it's only going to get harder. "If we're going to do something about bears, let's do it now while it's still easy."

When you start getting "distinguished lifetime achievement awards" (as he has), Chuck says, "What they're saying is 'Sit down, you're getting too damn old.'" But Chuck doesn't see it that way. He smiles: "After forty-four years, two months, and twenty-five days, I'm thinking of making it my life's work." ✦

Go east on Main Street, under the railroad overpass—watch for flooding if there's been heavy rain—and look for the building on the right with the life-size statue of an Indian and horse on the roof. That's where you'll find Kevin Eisele, the only custom boot maker within 141 miles of Miles City. Kevin's almost as much a landmark as the rooftop statues, holdovers from when the building housed the Coffrin photo gallery.

If you're satisfied with a pair of boots that might last through one cattle drive, Wal-Mart's got you covered, but if you're serious about your footwear, Eisele's Custom Boots is worth a trip to town. Kevin says, "It's not unusual for a pair of my boots to last ten years. The first pair I made was a packer-style lace-up for a fourteen-year-old, who eventually outgrew them, then handed them down."

This is no place for impulse buying: Plan to spend about an hour to have each foot carefully measured, which gets you placed on a two-year waiting list. Only Kevin does the measuring, and he guarantees the fit. "The boots should have a perfect fit instantly. They may need time for the leather to flex but they don't need to be 'broken in,'" he says. When your name comes up, you're on the way to happy feet, but "if a client has gained or lost weight or broken a foot, for example, I'll double-check the measurements before I begin cutting." He notes that feet flatten with age, and he factors in for swelling if he measures later in the day. Kevin doesn't do kids' boots because most folks wouldn't get their money's worth out of a pair that will be quickly outgrown. "Women are tough to fit because of swelling but they're not as vain as men," he says.

Boot making was a natural fit for Kevin. During a vacation from ranching, he went to school in Utah to learn the craft. It was a ranching accident, however, that gave Kevin a chance to

BOOT MAKER

KEVIN EISELE, MILES CITY

convert his interest into a career. He bought out a local boot repair and saddle business and began promoting his custom work through booths at the Bucking Horse Sale and craft fairs. Kevin's reputation for quality grew, and he quickly stood out from the twelve hundred custom bootmakers in the country and the handful in Montana. Initially he was located next to a funeral home. "I used to tell everyone that's where I got my leather," he jokes. He has already outgrown his fourth shop under the Indian and horse even though he's been there only a few years.

Kevin's not breaking new ground in how he makes boots, although the art of fitting has come a long way. "In the old days they used to make only one shape—no right or left. They'd soak them in water before putting them on so the boots would dry to fit," Kevin states. Some of his favorite work is for people with special foot problems—"they come first." He'll make an ankle-high lace-up for someone who needs extra support, an orthopedic shoe for a person with clubfoot, and boots via prescription for people with one leg shorter than another. It's all part of understanding how the boot will be used: "For cowboys, I ask what kind of stirrup they ride so I know how to cut the heels."

His boots are all leather, hand-stitched. Kevin boasts that you won't find any nails in them, either. Some materials he won't consider at all. "Snake won't stand up and it's too costly, and bison is too stretchy," he notes. Elephant hide is the toughest and along with ostrich is top-end, going for about $900 a pair, but locals don't request exotics, preferring calf leather instead. Although he'd like to buy American, he gets all of his leather through brokers who import from Europe. Their more durable leather is tanned with chromium sulfate, a process made cost-prohibitive in the United States by Environmental Protection Agency regulations. "When mad cow disease hit, the price shot up 15 percent," he says. Governmental interference doesn't stop there; Kevin needs a federal identification number just to buy his glue—it's considered a hazardous substance.

"There's $15 worth of materials in factory boots," he points out, but, "there's $175 in mine." He uses expensive leather, but that's not what drives up the price—it's the time and knowledge required to make them. He has eight to ten pairs in the works at a time, each involving about thirty hours of labor, although a pair he made for his wife, Patty, took nearly triple that, forty of it in tooling alone. "I always have a pair going for myself," he declares, adding that his are often made from scrap leather. "I enjoy the hand stitching; it's relaxing," he says, and it seems to suit his laid-back personality.

Comfortable boots are hard for some folks to part with no matter how torn up they get. As evidence, he points out a sad example on his repair shelf that are held together with yards of duct tape. "Those weren't made by me," Kevin laughs, adding, "There's nothing I can do to save them." A perfect example of why you pay more for handmade and why cheaper isn't always better.

Clients include local ranchers and hunters just passing through, but he has buyers all over the United States, including a lobbyist from Washington, D.C., a lawyer in San Francisco, and a commodities broker in Tennessee. A local rancher had his pair customized with the ranch's brand, and another pair was a hit at graduation when the student lifted his gown onstage to show them off, pants tucked into the boot tops.

Although boot making pays the rent, he's not in it strictly for the money: "When someone orders a second pair, you know they're happy." He sits down at one of the industrial-strength machines, tweaks a few settings, then picks up a piece of boot and begins stitching. Some lucky customer's number just came up. ✦

For many mountain climbers, reaching the summit inspires a moment of awe, solitude, and silence, but not Wayne Phillips—he can't keep his mouth shut. Anyone for miles will know he's there by his trademark yodel. "I need the right setting—a vista—to be inspired," he says. Reaching a mountaintop is just part of the fun; along the way Wayne carefully observes every leaf, flower, and fur ball he comes across. That's the nature of being a botanist—a yodeling wildflower botanist.

Wayne can't recall when he wasn't interested in natural history. As a kid he lived a block away from a huge college farm and loved to explore among the plants there. "My parents ran a restaurant and were busy all day, so this is how I entertained myself—it made me independent." He's also determined. As a Boy Scout he hiked the Pecos wilderness in less-than-ideal conditions with a guide who had a bad map. Although

things weren't going well, Wayne remembers thinking to himself, this is where I want to be. Their goal was to cross a tall mountain ridge, but deep snow forced them to go around it instead. "Fifty years later, with my son, I finished the trip the way we originally wanted to—over the top."

He's not sure whether it was the fact that he flunked algebra or aced botany, but he knew plant study would be his career and enrolled in forestry school at Texas A&M. He thought smoke-jumping (parachuting into wildfires) might be fun but was too young, and his father wouldn't sign the required permission papers, so Wayne took a summer job with the Forest Service in Idaho as part of a firefighting crew. While working a fire along the Lolo Trail, he became familiar with the plants of the Lewis and Clark expedition, which he would study and write about in detail years later. When he became old enough, he got his chance to smoke-

YODELING WILDFLOWER BOTANIST

WAYNE PHILLIPS, GREAT FALLS

jump for a couple years before graduating and heading off to northern Idaho to do "stand examination." Only a botanist would get excited about studying and assessing a plot of trees for harvesting and fire potential—its appeal for most people akin to watching moss grow—and Wayne was in his glory.

He was putting in as many as sixty-five hours a week without overtime, hazardous-duty pay, or comp time. "I didn't mind," he says. "I loved it and wanted my work to be good and done correctly." At times it was a life of isolation where grocery trips to Missoula or Spokane happened once a month. "Roughing it" meant donning snowshoes to do stand evaluations in the winter. He recalls a harrowing trip to rush his pregnant wife to the hospital three hours away on a bumpy, one-lane logging road. It's understandable that Wayne is rankled by the stereotype of government employees as unmotivated. "These people worked tirelessly because they enjoyed their jobs so much. We do this to manage the for-

est for the people." And he did it for thirty-three years, the last ten as an ecologist for the Lewis and Clark National Forest.

Like anyone with a passion, Wayne wants to share it, spread the word. In 1982 he found the perfect audience when he began teaching botany and wildflower classes at the Yellowstone Institute and later the Glacier Institute. Everyone from novices to PhDs comes to learn about medicinal and edible plants and feast on salads made from thistles, violets, and dandelions or take their turns cooking roots of American bistort and camas, but not until Wayne launches into a song or poem— "Them Botanists," a perennial crowd pleaser.

In fall lucky foragers dine on serviceberries, chokecherries, and four species of huckleberries. For those who would rather gawk than gobble, Wayne points out *Lewisia rediviva* (bitterroot), *Liatris pycnostachya* (tall blazing star), and *Xerophyllum tenax* (beargrass), but be forewarned: When he comes across a big tree, he bursts forth with his "If I Were a Tree" song, thrilling students and sending small animals hightailing it for cover. For the more adventurous, Wayne leads llama treks into the Beartooth Mountains. On one trip when a hiker became separated from the group, he took to yodeling to track her down. Whether her return to camp was through his efforts or her own sense of direction, the campfire discussion that evening centered on "emergency rescues and lessons learned that day," says Wayne.

Montana plants bring to mind prairie grasses and ponderosa pines; way down on the list is moss. Yet *Kelseya uniflora* (Kelsey's moss), a rare endemic, became the mascot for the Montana Native Plant Society. In the 1980s Wayne was part of a group of like-minded flora lovers that formed the society to "preserve, conserve, and educate people about the value of native plants and plant communities," and Wayne adds, "and just for fun." Wayne's idea of fun could fill a book—three of them, actually, the most recent being *Plants of the Lewis & Clark Expedition.*

Once word gets out that you're an expert on something, everyone wants a piece of you. Fortunately the Lewis and Clark Interpretive Center near his home in Great Falls had Wayne on its committee to assess plant mitigation. "They would have destroyed native plants during construction," he says. "I suggested we use those plants to landscape the visitor center." He collected seeds from thirty-three native plants to develop landscaping stock. Today visitors walk past Indian blanket, western wheatgrass, and golden currant, among others, thanks to Wayne. Lewis and Clark would be impressed.

Wayne's retired but not about to rest on his laurels. He has a goal: to climb the highest peak in each of Montana's mountain ranges. He keeps track of his conquests in a database and knows that he's yodeled on top of about two-thirds of them, already having scaled many of the more difficult ones. He's not sure when he'll top that final peak, but when it happens, everyone within earshot will know it. ◆

By day Eugene Edwards can be found sitting behind a desk working on dual degrees at the University of Montana. Although his days are full of studying math and elementary education, every so often he puts on his dancing clothes and hits the road, joining hundreds of other Native Americans on the powwow circuit. He says, "Cash prizes are an incentive, but it's not why I do it; I just love to perform. I've won some money dancing, but mostly I break even."

Powwows are a staple of Native American life throughout the United States, and Montana's no exception. It's a family reunion of sorts, a place to see old friends and make new ones. Eugene says, "It's a continuation of tradition; you keep yourself going." An outdoor powwow might seem more authentic, but from a practical standpoint, Eugene prefers to dance indoors: "Rain-drenched earth can make things bad for dancing and soak through moccasins."

POWWOW DANCER

EUGENE EDWARDS, BROWNING

Like most of the dancers, he started as a child, when he about five years old, "strongly urged" by his parents: "We were kids; we wanted to play." But he doesn't regret it now and in fact looks forward to each powwow, about fifteen a year, nearly all in the summer. He says that some of his teacher friends at the Blackfeet Head Start School at his home in Browning have taken sick leave during the school year to follow the competitions. Eugene has danced throughout the West, Southwest, Canada, and as far east as Nebraska. "We put on a lot of miles and we go through so many tires. The whole tribe hops into the car to save expenses," he says.

Even though his mother designs and makes his costumes, Eugene buys the necessary accessories. Fancy beaded moccasins and head-dresses that can put a Philadelphia Mummer to shame don't come cheap. Headgear such as a porcupine-hair roach (with two feathers attached so that they move in time with the dancer) can run $300 or more. Dancers' costumes are adorned with feathers, bone, claws, shells, and lots of colorful satin. A bird's-eye view of the dance floor sets to mind animated piñatas, color the predominant feature. But the color choices aren't random. For Eugene the purple and orange in his costume are family symbols; their design is the Rocky Mountain pattern, which features a zigzag of mountains in a diamond shape. Adding to the movement is foot-long yarn fringe that's attached to his costume's shoulders and bottom edge. Every year he gets a new outfit, each with the Edwards family purple and orange.

A powwow begins with the grand entry, a clockwise processional that follows an honor guard and includes all the dancers. Any age can participate; there's no maximum. "You can dance forever if you want," he notes. Men and women compete in traditional and fancy dances, but only men perform the grass dance, and it's women only in the jingle group. Categories accommodate everyone from toddlers to seniors. Eugene's specialty is the grass dance, which like all others is rich with Native lore. The fringe on his costume is symbolic of tall-prairie grass, and one story suggests that the dance replicates the movements of early hunters stalking game or the enemy. The dance also symbolizes life's harmony; steps danced on one leg must be repeated on the other.

Eugene creates his routine as he goes, "as the mood hits me." There's no set pattern, but the judges do look for creative footwork, costume, and enthusiasm. Of course you can't dance without music; each tribe has its own drum sound, along with a distinct style. Eugene says that music can influence how you perform: "There's some bad, some good," but the words aren't an issue because there aren't any. Vocables replace words of the old songs, which is just fine with Eugene because he doesn't speak his native language other than a few phrases.

When his grandmother died, Blackfeet tradition dictated that Eugene couldn't dance for one year. He also cut his hair, which "you do when any family member dies. After a year you can grow it back, but I prefer to keep mine short." As a result, he stands out from the crowd, sporting a buzz cut in sharp contrast with the long braids worn by most other men. It's customary that his grandmother give him his second (Native) name, but that now falls to Earl Old Person, tribal chief and Eugene's grandfather. In spite of having one degree and working toward others, he states, "I haven't achieved anything yet to get my second name."

The dance area is organized chaos, yet everyone seems to know what to do next. As in any healthy competition, there's rivalry, and Eugene points out that the hosting tribe has the edge on winning. But it doesn't really matter—competitors are in it for the love of dancing, which often goes on until midnight or longer. Dances are periodically interrupted by a giveaway ceremony that honors an individual.

If Eugene had to pick just one powwow to go to, it would be the Julyamish in Post Falls, Idaho, because "it's large and there's lots going on," including a traditional basketball tournament, "where you can win jackets, money, and trophies." In Montana the big one is Crow Fair in August, when Crow Agency turns into the "tepee capital of the world," but he has a bias toward Native American Indian Days in Browning. "The parade is the largest in Montana, and my family's float has won first prize two years in a row."

It's a shame that many Montanans have never been to a powwow, considering it's such a huge part of our state's heritage. The dances are public, and anyone—including non-Natives—can join in the noncompetitive intertribal dancing. Even those who can't carry a tune or have two left feet will at least be tapping along to the drumbeat. And you might run into an old friend . . . or make a new one. ✦

It could be called Montana's bee belt—this agricultural area stretching roughly from Laurel to Custer to Pryor. Each summer fields of lush green alfalfa are dotted with what appear to be school-bus shelters, only these are painted various colors with symbols or patterns on their sides. HI, A4, flowers, polka dots, or checkerboards may not mean much to a passerby but to the resident leaf-cutter bees, it's home. These are special tenants, and since 1987 Jack Roan has been their landlord.

LEAF-CUTTER BEEKEEPER

JACK ROAN, CUSTER

Ordinarily leaf-cutters would be considered plant-damaging pests and evicted as quickly as possible. But these are the good guys, used to pollinate alfalfa, and to keep his seasonal workers productive, he provides room and board. According to Jack, "This alfalfa is grown for seed, and better pollination equals better yield."

Managing this workforce is a year-round job, and to get the most out of them, timing is everything. To coincide with flowering, Jack wants to have his one hundred or so sheds in the field by late June. Then under cover of darkness he puts trays of bees into the buildings. There's nothing clandestine about it: "Bees don't fly if the temperature is less than 70 degrees, which is why I put them out at night," he says.

But pollination is only half their job—the other half is to lay eggs to perpetuate his stock. Spitting up wads of regurgitated leaves to build a nest is appealing only to the bees and, of course, Jack. To provide nesting sites, he places an ammo crate with "bee boards" in each shed. The boards have long holes bored into them where the bees lay their eggs in long, tubelike cocoons. In the morning when it warms up, they come to life and head out to begin pollinating and working the fields. As they flit from plant to plant, they gather the material needed to take back to the sheds and build their egg casings. The bees live only six to eight weeks, but their eggs are safe within the leaf-matter cocoons that Jack brings in from the fields.

Just how many bees does it take to create prime alfalfa seed? "Lots," says Jack. He calculates there are three thousand eggs per ammo box and ten thousand bees per gallon; he uses about two to three gallons per acre, and he's working 400 acres: That translates to a whole bunch of bees, about eight million actually. Originally he bought his stock in Canada for $200 a gallon, but today after figuring out how many eggs he'll need for the following season, he sells off the excess.

In the corner of a climate-controlled warehouse in center-city Custer sit rows of garbage cans filled with eggs and their casings. How they got there is another part of Jack's operation. "The eggs don't just magically fall out of the huts," he jokes. The bee boards are marked on top and grooved so that when they are face-to-face (like slices of bread in a loaf), they have holes the length of each board. Back at the warehouse, the boards

are popped apart, then run through a machine that removes the long rods and breaks them into individual egg casings about the size of rabbit pellets. They're finally ready to be tucked in for the winter, relaxing contentedly in cold metal cans. Come summer Jack warms them to hatching, then puts them in the huts to begin the cycle again.

During the off-season he makes repairs or builds new sheds. It's pretty straightforward work; the most creative part is deciding what to put on the outside. He says one beekeeper's wife paints little pictures on their sheds but he's less artistic, preferring to mark them with letters and numbers. He admits the symbols may or may not matter—bees can't read the markings—what's important is that each shed is different from the other, so the bees can return to the same one each time. They get oriented to other things like trees, and if you move the shed a little, they'll still find it. "But if you move it a great distance, or remove it, they'll come back to the spot where the shed was and hang around looking for it." In summer he loads the refurbished buildings onto the modified bed of his pickup to plunk them down in the fields.

Just because they're insects doesn't mean they're immune from the government's red tape. The eggs must be inspected by the state, so Jack sends the inspectors a cup of the critters, which are x-rayed to determine how many of the nests are active. He laughs as he tells about a bee rustler who stole another beekeeper's herd and was caught when he sent them in for testing. The insects also are not immune to disease and parasites. The most feared is chalkbrood, an intestinal fungal infection. To control it Jack bakes the bee boards in a huge oven he built specifically for the purpose and dips the larvae in bleach before drying them.

Although he puts in long days, he claims to be semiretired, which in Jack language means he's scaled down to servicing only a few select clients and working fewer acres. This leaves time to attend the annual Leaf-Cutter Bee Convention in either Reno or Las Vegas to inspect the newest equipment, see old friends, and learn about new techniques, and maybe drop just a quarter or two.

Jack and his bees help farmers get more bang for their buck—more alfalfa per acre. Though not ranking up there with cattle or sheep in importance, they have their place in Montana's economy—problem is they're a little difficult to see; if it weren't for their sheds, you'd never know they were here. And even though they don't have stingers, Jack says, "they do bite, and you don't want to get them mad." There's nothing worse than a cross pollinator. ◆

Loma's one of those northern prairie towns in the Big Open that's easy to miss. Its lone business is the cafe on a main street that passes through town on its way to somewhere else. The entire residential section lies to the east on gravel streets, the majority of its population residing in Marion Britton's household in downtown Loma. A hand-painted sign above the door on a little white house reads: DOLL MUSEUM, HOUSE OF 1,000 DOLLS, one of the two museums in this quaint, lopsided village. There used to be a small faded sign along the main highway, too, but Marion took it down, explaining, "Hours are by appointment only. I'm not as able to keep it open the way I used to." That doesn't mean she's not delighted to give tours.

Marion warns, "Collecting is like a disease—either you catch it or you don't." It starts with one item, then another, and pretty soon you're obsessed. That's pretty much the case with

---

DOLL COLLECTOR

MARION BRITTON, LOMA

Marion, whose collection began with her own doll, although she notes, "I didn't really play much with dolls as a girl; I played with the farm animals and horses on our homestead near Havre." But she was fond of dolls and as word grew was given them as gifts. "Bachelor homesteaders took a liking to the local kids since they didn't have children of their own. They frequently gave us things, sometimes dolls." Although she was born December 23, she was lucky: "I usually got two presents," one of them a doll. And so it began.

Dolls didn't always come to her. Marion admits, "I'm a cheapskate, and shows offered the best prices, better than buying off the street or from people coming to my shop." She used to go to Seattle on buying trips, boarding the train in Havre. "I could get there by 8:00 A.M.—after riding all night—go to the doll show, then catch the evening train to be home the next morning."

Although the trip was a two-day affair, it was made just a bit easier because her husband was an ex-railroader, so she had a pass, leaving more spending money for her pursuit. She notes, "I once went to Cincinnati to a show, too," that one by bus.

After retiring as a schoolteacher, her son gave her the building in Loma to use as a museum. Until then dolls were all over her house, more than one thousand at last count. Whether for display or just to have a place to sit, her son built shelves to house her collection. Now Marion had a new title: museum curator. There's no admission charge and she doesn't request a donation, although there is a jar by the door for those inclined to leave something. But she does ask that you sign her guest book, which records visitors from Idaho Falls, San Diego, Pittsburgh, and exotic locales like Bozeman and Saudi Arabia—"I don't know how they ever found me," she exclaims.

She once gave a tour to a small group that she thought was unusually quiet: "They didn't have any questions or comments." When she checked the sign-in book, she discovered they were European and wondered if they spoke English. "I don't think they understood a word I said, but they seemed to enjoy themselves."

Dolls are everywhere, some in special settings with furniture and accessories. With the memory of an elephant, she can rattle off any doll's name, where she acquired it, and who gave it to her. A tin-headed resident is her oldest, dating from 1839. Social butterflies Barbie and Ken represent the more recent end of the spectrum, although nothing is newer than the 1970s: "That's where I stopped." Her family comes in all materials: china, celluloid, metal, chalk, cloth, and wood. Bisque dolls were too delicate to play with, so those with metal heads tend to be more banged up. An old bisque is her favorite, but Barbie predecessor Amy comes in a close second.

Marion's largest doll stands 3 feet tall, and at half an inch, the smallest—a Kewpie—is easy to miss. She knows the history of each. "The Kewpie was created by Rose O'Neil, who wrote and illustrated for *Ladies' Home Journal* and named them after Cupid. They eventually became popular as carnival giveaways." The Indian Skookum doll (*Skookum* is Canadian Chinook for "really good") was patented by a woman in Missoula in the early 1900s. Her Poor Pitiful Pearl was based on a cartoon character and issued in the late 1950s; she's dressed in rags with the idea that her owner can transform her from pitiful to pretty. Marion laments she has only one of the Dionne quints: "They're hard to find."

Collectors often become experts. When word got out about Marion, she was asked to identify a doll's head found in a latrine at Fort Benton when refurbishing the fort. She had one just like it and identified it as a covered wagon doll—owned by girls who came west on wagon trains.

Marion has not only dolls but also some of the original boxes, and as anyone who's watched *Antiques Roadshow* knows, that's where the value lies. But the boxes aren't on display—no room. Also packed away is some of the old clothing. It's fragile, so she made reproductions to outfit her crew. She doesn't "play" with the dolls when no one is around but does enjoy looking at them and imagining what was going on in the world at the time that doll was in use and "what the child's life was like who owned it."

"The dolls get more valuable as they get older—I don't," she quips. However, Marion has no intentions of selling the collection: "My son will take it over." But some dolls are priceless, such as the one her grandmother gave her. "She put a Bible quote with it that read, 'Be ye thankful for what you have.' " And Marion is, a thousand times over. ◆

A monster in Flathead Lake—some find it easier to believe than Bigfoot, UFOs, or a democratic governor in Montana. Laney Hanzel, Flathead Lake expert, says there just might be such a creature, but he hasn't seen one—the monster, that is, not the governor. That doesn't mean other people haven't. A retired army colonel says he saw it twice—once in 1985 at Yellow Bay and again in 1987 in a completely different spot. He describes something 3 to 4 feet in diameter, 20 to 30 feet long, with steely black eyes, and that undulated through the water.

FLATHEAD LAKE CREATURE EXPERT

LANEY HANZEL, KALISPELL

Like most people Laney has been skeptical of these reports. But a well-known cryptozoologist (one who studies monsters and sea creatures) said that every large body of water in the world has claims of some sort of creature, so Laney decided he'd better treat the colonel's sightings more seriously. He notes, "I hesitate to use the word *monster* [as the first reports in 1889 did] in describing this thing because it suggests that it has acted in some sinister, evil way. None of the accounts state that kind of activity, so I prefer to call it the Flathead Lake creature."

He didn't set out to be the say-so on the USO (unidentified swimming object)—it just happened. It pretty much started in 1966 when his employer, the Department of Fisheries, had him out on the lake assessing the fish population. Because he spent nearly 90 percent of his time around the water, it was only natural that he'd hear all kinds of monster stories. A blurb in the local paper mentioned that Laney would be collecting information on the creature. Within a week his phone started ringing. Digging deeper, he found that Paul Fugleberg, editor of the Polson newspaper, had been keeping records, too, and decided there needed to be a clearinghouse for such reports—and Laney was it.

Like any good monster tracker, Laney scoured the earliest reports for sightings. He found that on a Sunday paddleboat trip in 1889, more than one hundred passengers saw something sticking out of the water, swimming with serpentlike motions. That was the beginning: To date there have been more than seventy sightings, most on calm waters, which is an important detail because mirages can occur in rough water.

Most witnesses are reluctant to admit they've seen this Nessie of the North, which Laney feels further substantiates their credibility. "At least eight people I know well and trust have filed reports even though they didn't want to go public with it. They're not looking for publicity." In fact he holds people's names in confidence: "All I want to do is collect facts." He asks uncoached questions to make sure the reports aren't influenced by newspaper accounts.

In one case a visiting policeman and his family watched the creature for more than five minutes from their boat and could describe it in detail. From a bluff a doctor and her son, a marine biologist, watched the creature for forty-five minutes. Two women and their kids saw two monsters, one smaller than the other, at the same time: This suggested a parent with young. Laney says that means there must be at least three in the lake. It also explains how a monster could still be present after all these years—it's breeding.

Some details in the reports have almost made Laney a believer: "I'm hearing things that are not public knowledge." Specifically, many people observed that before the creature appeared, there was a "spritzing" on the surface, the kind of activity that happens when schools of small fish rise out of the water to avoid being eaten by a larger fish. He knew this wasn't something observers had read about in other Flathead Lake monster reports.

Flathead is the largest natural freshwater lake west of the Mississippi, so to keep track of the creature's whereabouts, Laney created a map (www.flatheadlakers.org) that conveniently combines graphics and data. His notations show the creature surfacing in shallower waters. Study the map carefully and you'll notice that the lake legend was spotted on opposite sides of the lake within twenty-five minutes of each other, which means either there's more than one or this guy can swim 60 miles an hour. Even further scrutiny shows one appearance was witnessed by more than one person from slightly different locations at the same time. Hmmmm . . .

Some years there are no reported appearances, others just a few. Laney's bar chart shows the number of creature and large fish sightings by year: In 1993 the big guy was seen in more places than Elvis. "I checked with Fugleberg. Turns out combined we had thirteen separate reports, but since then there have been just two or three. There's no account for why they suddenly went down after 1993."

In all his years on the fisheries boat, he's not seen any sign of the monster, even with the aid of his supercharged fish finder that can detect a 1-inch fish 300 feet down. With all his high-tech equipment he's identified sunken airplanes and found a couple of human bodies, but still no monster, yet he says, "I can't help feeling something's out there."

Fact or fiction, there's money in monsters. In just about any tourist trap within 50 miles of the lake you'll find monster T-shirts, caps, burgers, and—the creature would be so proud—beer. A national tabloid ran the story about a child who fell into the lake and was saved by the creature. The underwater denizen is also responsible for Laney's fifteen minutes of fame: a segment on the TV show *Strange Universe*.

Laney retired in 1993, but his days are filled with keeping tabs on this mysterious fauna of Flathead Lake. Asked whether he believes the monster exists, he says it's hard to dispute all of the evidence: "I've never seen the creature, but I've had some awfully big holes in my net." ◆

Most cowboys aren't wowed by an Armani suit. Rolex means nothing to them. And a BMW will generate a yawn. But if you have your butt parked on a Ben Swanke saddle, now that's something. From the Ben Swanke Saddle Co. come some of the best saddles to top a horse. Step into this low-profile shop in east Billings, and the first thing you notice is the familiar smell of leather and how clean the place is. Saddles in various stages of completion are parked all over the room.

Be forewarned that there's no buying off the rack here; everything is custom-made, so it will be a while before you claim bragging rights and become the envy of all your friends. Placing an order can take as little as five minutes if the saddle seeker knows what he or she wants or an entire day if he or she comes in without a clue and needs Ben's input. He's glad to give it but likes when people know what they want: "Too much open creativity is a little scary."

SADDLEMAKER

BEN SWANKE, BILLINGS

Ben's not slow, he's thorough, and even with his wife, Pam, and an assistant to help, it takes time to produce an heirloom. But he crafts more than just a pretty saddle; it's what's on the inside—the tree—that helps make his special. A lot of other saddlemakers use commercially manufactured trees; however, Ben makes his by hand. "Just as a good house has a solid foundation, a fine saddle needs a quality tree," he notes.

Only about a half-dozen people in the United States make them, and in fact Ben's trees are so highly regarded, he builds them for other saddlemakers. Ben says his are better because he uses grade perfect (the best and clearest) poplar and birch, unlike some who use knotty wood. It's an engineering fact that laminated wood—as his trees are—is stronger than one solid piece.

Designing a saddle is tough enough, but picking the right tree can be downright confusing, and Ben will need to know how the saddle will be used to help you pick out the best one. No matter what style—the Will James, Nevada Slick, Pryor Creek Special, Bull Moose, among many others—the process is the same and takes several days to weeks if you want a thoroughly cured one, and why wouldn't you? He cuts, glues, and rough cuts the wooden tree before sanding it to perfection, then gives it two coats of polyurethane.

When you open the freezer in Ben's shop, don't expect to find bratwurst—his is full of bull rawhide that he buys frozen to keep it fresh. The trees are wrapped in damp rawhide tacked in place to retain the contour of the tree. "This gives it about 80 percent of its strength" and adds to the earthy aroma in Ben's shop. It's then laced with deer rawhide before getting a final coat of poly to seal all the seams and stitches. "This," he says, "prevents water from entering, not that it happens a lot but some horses may be forced to swim, getting the saddle wet," which can be real hard on it. He's proud to say he's done few repairs on his own cre-

ations, of which he's made more than one thousand since 1980.

Ben started playing with leather and saddles when he was fourteen. He made the first one for himself but later sold it for about $300 because he needed the money. "It was pretty rough compared to what I do now," and what he does now ranks up there with fine art.

Maybe it's the hand tooling, which can cover nearly every inch, to a plain style with barely any handwork. Perhaps it's the overall quality of quarter-inch-thick leather expertly stitched that makes Ben's style stand out, so much so that, "More than one of my customers said they can spot my saddles anywhere, like the guys who were hunting in the Big Hole and recognized one." And it's not just because he signs them.

To the trained eye, like a fine antique, a saddle can be dated by the cantle (back) style or the leather's color. "Cantles are high now and you can barely give away one made with a low back," but Ben's hold their value and have actually increased over time. "I've seen my saddles sell at auction for more than their original cost. I couldn't believe it."

Ben does all he can to make sure that a saddle leaves his shop in mint condition and cringes at the cowboy who has just paid $2,800 or more for one that he throws into the back of a pickup loaded with barbwire, but he smiles knowingly when a new owner brings a special blanket to cushion and protect his. Ben's fond of saying, "A good saddle will squeak forever," but that's assuming it sees the back of a horse; some people buy them as showpieces only and sell them as works of art.

Pick up one of Ben's catalogs and drool over the photos but don't expect Santa to bring you one this Christmas—or the next. Even though Ben has about five saddles in the works at one time, there's at least a two-year waiting list, so plan carefully. He does do repairs, depending on how badly you need your saddle returned, but will turn you away if you show up with a broken purse strap or torn belt: "I simply don't have the time for it." He will consider making chaps or a rifle scabbard but only to match a buyer's new saddle.

Ben's work is in demand, from the East Coast where western-style saddles are gaining in popularity to the customer in Canada who's quoted in the Swanke catalog: "You can ride this rig all week, go to a roping on Saturday, and she's fancy enough to go to church on Sunday." Boy, howdy. ✦

Everyone was sure Sammy was lost in the forest and had died. But one day Michelle Feldstein saw the thirty-year-old palomino running loose along the road near her ranch in Paradise Valley. Sammy was a retired National Park Service horse that used to carry water to rangers in the backcountry. Michelle was given permission to keep him for the summer, but at the end of the season the park service told her they were required to dispose of animals by auctioning them off, so she found herself in Billings bidding against canners. Sammy moved in with Michelle and husband, Al, and she and the family dog spent Sammy's first night sleeping nearby in the camper to keep an eye on him. He received his own bucket and personalized sign, was put on supplements, and thrived for another four years. She notes, "Sammy was the first horse buried on our property."

There's a similar story behind Beasty, Thumbellina, Tain, Beauty, Bozo, and Finean—just

ANIMAL RESCUER

MICHELLE FELDSTEIN, LIVINGSTON

a few of Michelle's rescues. On the 270-acre ranch south of Livingston, life is good for her three dogs, thirty-two cats, fourteen llamas, twenty-three chickens, forty-two equines, and counting. Michelle is emphatic that she's not competing with the humane society and doesn't accept kittens, puppies, and abandoned Easter bunnies but instead takes in the hard-to-place geriatric and special-needs animals. Michelle gets emotional talking about Daisy the cow, who, at twenty-three years old, came to live at the ranch because her owner was too old to take care of her. She lived comfortably for another two years. "She was a wonderful cow."

Michelle and Al came to Paradise Valley in 1990, falling in love with Deer Haven Ranch at first sight. The guesthouse was perfect for her daughter, but little did Michelle realize that later it would help fund the enormous medical and food bills her menagerie would generate. At $1,000 a month for the veterinarian, she probably gets a real nice Christmas card each year, and the local feed mills are always glad to see her. "My vet bill each month is a given, and the farrier comes for two days at a time." Neither could she know how much work it would take to tend the flock: "I spend two hours each day just cleaning up." But she's not complaining.

Michelle has never had to go looking for new tenants; they find her. She has a hard time saying no, especially to the hard-luck cases. Deer Haven started out like a typical ranch: three healthy horses, a dog, and one cat, but "my daughter was working at the humane society, and before long our cat population grew." Word got out, and soon older and larger animals showed up. Oliver, a huge white horse, was headed toward the glue factory because he was prone to seizures when she took him in. Stormy wasn't in much better shape; he was four hundred pounds underweight and wasn't expected to live two weeks. "I got three hundred pounds back on him in no time," largely through

her research and use of supplements, vitamins, and minerals, which she swears by.

The views of the Yellowstone River and Absaroka Mountains grab your attention when you enter the house, but only until you realize you're surrounded—by cats, lots of cats. However, this is only part of the group; the rest are lounging in the heated tack room in the barn, where they have their own couch. Once accepted, all of Michelle's cats are spayed or neutered, but many of them have issues. "Princess was abused and has social problems. We don't ask much of her; she relaxes in front of her own fan now." It becomes obvious after watching Michelle serve as a doorman that there are no cat doors in the house, and for good reason. "They bring in critters," and her hospitality stops at snakes. She wouldn't hurt one, "but they aren't welcome."

At her guesthouse, people *are* welcome, with one provision: "You must like animals," and she means it. Michelle screens paying guests through phone conversations and doesn't accept tourists off the road or one-nighters. It's not a bed-and-breakfast; Michelle doesn't cook but keeps the pantry stocked and provides eggs from her flock of chickens, acquired through the local classifieds: "These birds were destined for table fare, now they're providing it." But not all guests sleep in—kids staying with their parents often volunteer to help clean the corrals. Word of mouth, the family Web site (www.alfeldstein.com), and Al generate the revenue to keep the Feldstein ark afloat.

Although she's careful about who rents, she's even more particular about the occasional house sitter. "My trust factor of humans is very thin. I need someone who gets as much comfort out of taking care of my animals as I do. They need to check them every day for cuts or bruises, clean the stalls, and give them the love and attention I would." She has horror stories to tell and won't hesitate to fire anyone who doesn't work out.

The toughest thing for Michelle is having to put an animal down. "It never gets easier, no matter how many you have, but I want my animals to die with dignity. Even when they're buried I won't allow them to be dragged; they must be carefully placed in the ground," she says, adding, "Grief isn't limited to humans. I've seen horses mourn."

She gently pats the ranch's celebrity, Ima—as in "I'm a horse"—who pulled the doctor's carriage in *A River Runs Through It*. "There was so much wrong with this horse that the vet told his owner to euthanize him, but he's still here and in fact has taught all my grandchildren to ride." Sharing the pasture with Ima, burros, donkeys, miniature horses, and Shetlands is Lady, a forty-year-old pony bought at auction by someone wanting to play a joke on a friend. After the joke wore off, no one wanted her. Thanks to Michelle, she's now in paradise, having the last laugh. ◆

Some folks won't finalize their summer vacation plans to Flathead Lake until they've checked with Barry Flamm. He doesn't book flights, provide lodging, or offer backcountry tours—Barry grows cherries, and when the picking is right, these fruit fans want to be near Polson. His orchard isn't the largest in the Flathead; it's not the oldest, either. But it is the only certified organic cherry operation in the state, and he has the framed document to prove it. Although there are other certified organic farmers in Montana, Barry's got the corner on cherries.

Growing up in Ohio in the days of industrialization—when the Cuyahoga River caught fire—he had an interest in nature before *environment* became a buzzword. A trip out West with his father motivated him to head to Colorado as soon as he got out of high school. "It wasn't until I moved out there that I realized that not everyone had black

ORGANIC CHERRY GROWER

BARRY FLAMM, POLSON

snot," he jokes, referring to Ohio's then-polluted air.

While earning his degree in forestry from Colorado State, he spent summers logging and doing ranch work, landing a job with the Forest Service after graduation. Ten years later he was director of the Shoshone National Forest in Wyoming, at thirty-one, the youngest forest supervisor in the nation.

That didn't keep him out of Vietnam, but he didn't mind. As part of the green revolution, Barry volunteered to do forest assessment in Vietnam, following a similar program in the Philippines. It looked as though the war was winding down, but the Tet offensive changed everything, and Barry found himself studying the Asian jungles at the worst time. Even as a civilian, he soon realized that his job as a forester had changed dramatically. "It was clear the military was destroying the forest, yet we were there to restore and maintain it."

In Vietnam Barry saw firsthand the effects of pesticides. The landscape was showered with barrels of the defoliant 2,4-D and 2,4,5-T, aka Agent Orange, from spray planes code-named Ranch Hand. Special Forces maintained spraying wasn't working as a military technique (the French didn't agree and complained that deforestation was ruining their rubber plants, in particular, Michelin tires). "The military looked forward and still saw trees. If they would have looked up they'd have noticed the canopy was missing. Everyone there was ignorant about dioxin. I was well exposed but had no concerns at the time."

Back in Washington, D.C., Barry was in charge of developing environmental policy under Presidents Nixon, Ford, and Carter, resigning during the Reagan administration. After the National Environmental Policy Act was passed, he went back to the Department of Agriculture and established the Office of Environmental Quality, where he was responsible for every aspect of environmental quality. "This cemented my feelings about the virtues of organic farming," but Barry still had bigger cherries to pick before growing his own.

While he was conducting a study in Central and South America, the Wilderness Society gave him the title of chief forester and asked him to write a policy to present to the U.S. government as a better forest plan. Six years later he wrapped it up and left for Nepal to head the forest policy program there (the average person would have had their fill of trees, but Barry later developed a similar plan in China).

On his way back to Washington from Nepal, Barry detoured through Montana. He'd been here often, backpacking and fishing. "I loved the Flathead area the most and knew someday I'd move here. I wanted a place to practice some of my preaching about organic farming and forestry management." He practices cherries—a difficult crop—and preached his way onto the advisory committee that helped establish the organic certification program in Montana.

Defining *organic* could a fill a book, but the bottom line is it means a different approach to growing crops. Independent testing labs in Oregon ensure that standards under the National Organic Act are met—the EPA keeps an eye out, too. Everything from pest and disease control to fertilization must be chemical free. Regular agriculture has no standards for how many pesticides are used.

Naturally all this healthy produce comes at a cost—to organic growers and consumers. To rid his few apple trees of codling moths, Barry spends $200 on parasitic wasps, which have no loyalty or regard for his property line and take off after their job is done. For further control he plants disease-resistant species. We may not understand biological botanicals, pyrethrums, or soil bacteria extracts, but Barry does, and he knows they're very expensive, one of them running $330 a pound. Fertilizer is cheaper—he plants his own, growing chemical-free green manure like legumes, winter rye, clover, and buckwheat.

At barely fifteen acres Barry's operation is average for a Flathead Lake orchard, but his trees have wonderful views of the peaks in Glacier Park to the north and Flathead's southern shore. Still it's a lot for one guy to handle. Most of his one thousand trees were planted after he lost a bunch during a hard freeze. His days are long and spent maintaining a favorable environment for six varieties of cherries and eight types of apples. He prunes all the trees by hand. "What I don't grind into mulch I burn for firewood," he says.

Barry's cherries are in demand at food co-ops from Great Falls to Whitefish, but many go to tourists and locals who are happy to pay 85 cents a pound to pick the fruit themselves. For those who prefer fast food, he sells already-picked cherries on-site. In addition to repeat clients—many who plan their vacations around his crop—he also welcomes study groups who want to learn the finer points of organic farming. "You want cherries that still have stems on so there's no sap loss and less chance of spoilage," he says. "Our cherries are noted for being organic and their high quality and great taste. I let the fruit speak for itself." ◆

It's early morning in Bozeman, and Tom Wolfe has a date with Thelma and Louise. He greets them at the door. They silently follow him across the hard rubber floor to the other side of the room, where he ties them up and begins to remove their shoes. These ladies are big, beautiful, Belgian draft horses, and Tom is their farrier.

Although several glowing forges and at least a dozen anvils line the perimeter of the large, open workroom, this is not a typical blacksmithing operation. It's Montana State University's horseshoeing school, and Tom, a Great Falls native, is the teacher. A local professional and one of Tom's students are helping to reshoe not only the gentle Thelma and Louise but also Bert and Ernie. These Belgian behemoths need more extensive work than your average packhorse, so Tom and his crew will be at it all day.

But go back to the late 1960s when Tom was a college graduate looking for his first teaching

<hr />

FARRIER

TOM WOLFE, BOZEMAN

<hr />

job. He landed instead a position as counselor at a small college. At a career day he watched a shoeing demonstration and thought this work might make a good summer sideline; besides, he really liked horses. Also appealing was the idea of being his own boss, working with iron, and being able to get started with little investment. "So, with no horse background, I took a course, apprenticed, and then shod for a living for twelve years. When the job opened as a teacher at MSU, I jumped at it."

Tom's students are not traditional by any means: The average age is thirty-one, most come for a career change, 90 percent are from out of state, and shoeing is usually totally unrelated to what they had been doing. What sets them apart even more is that they come for three months at a time and put in eight-hour days. Hardly your typical college student, these folks attend for the experience rather than credits. For that matter the whole course is nontraditional in that it receives no state funding and is completely self-supporting. "But we get a great deal of nonfinancial support from the university," Tom adds proudly. The class is maintained solely through tuition and the $20 or so they charge customers for materials (an outside professional will run you $75 to $250).

Class size is about ten students (35 percent of his graduates are women). Today the horses have come to them, but usually Tom and the gang hit the road, servicing everything from dude ranches to working ranches. Recreation and tourism account for a large part of the 35,000 horses in the Gallatin Valley, home to one of the highest concentrations in the state. That translates to 140,000 hooves, which is more than Tom and the county's eight or nine full-time farriers can handle. He laments, "I've had to turn away as much work as I take."

Tom really loves teaching. "I never felt like it was a job or going to work—I feel a little guilty about that," he says, grinning. With his collection of more than one hundred horseshoes as a back-drop, he instructs his class on the horse anatomy and physiology that would-be farriers need to know to work on-site with a vet so they can make the proper shoe. And making corrective shoes is what Tom's known for (he notes that the term *corrective shoe* isn't used much anymore and instead is referred to as "shoeing for lameness"). It was because of his reputation that the humane society contacted him with what has become his most bizarre case. A team of ponies that were kept in a deep, muddy pen had developed hooves so long that they curled back against themselves, actually rubbing the front of the shin. But the story has a happy ending: "We fixed them up and a local woman adopted them."

As Tom files Thelma's hooves, he explains that shoes are for prevention and protection. Like for people, different shoes are for different purposes, depending on how the horse is used—hauling, trail riding, or ranching, for example. Whether from genetics or abuse, lameness is common, which is why the farrier is critical to ranch life.

"The work is physical but very rewarding," Tom says as he recalls some of his customers. He stresses that being a good horseshoer includes knowing how to handle the horse as well as its owner. "The meanest horse I ever worked on was part of a draft team in the Tetons—it was large and ill-mannered." But some are so nice that they voluntarily lift their feet when he works on them. He has had some bad human customers, too, but "you only need to see them for a few hours every eight weeks, which is how often the horses must be shod. Most owners are great and often give us coffee and cookies, even an occasional meal."

When he's not next to a horse, Tom presents seminars on his craft. "Techniques haven't changed too much over the years, but the tools have—much better quality and more specific to their function. Ergonomics especially is a big thing." Shoes have evolved as well. Although the majority are still steel or aluminum, some synthetics have appeared, and others have built-in traction devices. But the method remains the same: Take a shoe, heat it red hot, hammer it on an anvil to fit the horse's foot, then nail it in place. Nailing, in fact, doesn't hurt the horse but there isn't much room for error, $\frac{1}{4}$ inch or less, which is where the farrier's skill comes in.

Has he ever been kicked? "No. You get to know horses and read the one you're working on—I've been stepped on often enough, though." But it won't happen today.

Thelma has stood patiently for hours, at times almost offering her foot to Tom. He puts the finishing touches on her new pair of high-end shoes, gives her an affectionate pat on the rump, then turns his attention to Louise. ◆

Like many Montanans, Larry Evans hunts. Come spring he dons outdoor clothing, grabs a sack, and heads off to the woods in search of his favorite prey. He never worries that his scent or footsteps will scare off the quarry—it's not going anywhere. Other hunters, some only yards away, present an almost eerie scene as they quietly and methodically move through the forest, eyes intent on the ground. Larry bends down and gently plucks a wrinkled brown cone-shaped fungus from the leaf litter. He bags the trophy, then goes on for the next. They're all looking for the same thing—morel mushrooms, big game for fungus lovers everywhere, and Larry is an expert, a mycologist.

Montana is ripe for the picking, in large part because of its forest fires. "The best place to find them is burned-over areas," Larry says. Morels are the Cadillac of mushrooms, prized by restaurants and gourmands for their flavor and texture, and they're

MYCOLOGIST

LARRY EVANS, MISSOULA

one of the easiest to safely identify in the wild. "They can be cultivated but those taste terrible, and it's not cost-effective commercially," he notes.

Of course anything that good comes with a price, and these fungal delights aren't cheap, commanding hundreds of dollars a pound. Commercial harvesters are required to get a permit; casual fungal fans may pick gratis but must cut their 'shrooms in half to make them less marketable. Competition is fierce and urban legends abound: More than one Forest Service employee tells stories of gunfire and violence in the woods. Local newspapers frequently run features about conflicts, but Larry says he hasn't had a problem with "mushroom-jackers," although "there are some low-baggers out there picking."

He feels a bigger problem is that the mushrooms are picked too early, taking the minis and not allowing them to mature. The season is measured in days: "You usually get a sixty-day harvest time once every three or four years, but it depends on the weather—sometimes it's only thirty days." He'd like to see a fixed season that's legally enforced. The Forest Service monitors patches as best it can, but outside buyers try to scare off the locals so they can get their crews in to pick.

There are about a dozen varieties of morels, but the most common to Montana are the blacks, grays, and yellows: "Most desired are the blacks and grays but they all taste pretty much the same." Not only morels, but also Montana truffles, chanterelles, oysters, even the lowly puffball, which tastes great fried in butter, are highly prized. Larry says, "Fungi are the predominant life form on a microscopic level but even though a handful of soil yields millions of mycelia, there's no guarantee anything will sprout—you need the right conditions."

Conditions were right in Illinois, where Larry grew up and his interest in mushrooms was fostered by his mother. Armed with a botany degree and a minor in microbiology from the University of Montana, he spent time in Korea teaching English. Then after hunting mushrooms in Russia—"They take it much more seriously there"—he returned to Missoula to run a restaurant for a few years, creating gourmet dishes and selling fungi: "I got the state's first mushroom vending certification."

Larry divides his time between summers at the farmers' market selling mushrooms and teaching at the university and Glacier Institute, where fungal fanatics sign up for "Spring Mushroom Extravaganza" and "Fall Mushroom Roundup" and delight in mycology taste tests. Larry stresses, however, "You can't learn everything from a book," which has led to his founding the Western Montana Mycological Association (WMMA). And several hundred members agree, some joining because of Larry's reputation and others using it as a support group for their passion and maybe just to find the best spots for morels. He's on the must-call list for the Rocky Mountain Poison Control Network, who treat folks who've been poisoned because they "tried to trip on mushrooms" or misidentified them. "The most common error is stories with mislabeled photos. You've especially got to be careful of false morels."

Because of Larry, morel munchers everywhere can forage more safely. Through the WMMA Web site (www.fungaljungal.org)—almost a mycology course in itself—there's a complete photo library to aid with identification or any other aspect of mushroom mania. If you have a craving for mushroom pierogies, the recipe's here. Maybe you're in the market for a fungal T-shirt. Perhaps videos are more your speed: For 27 minutes you'll be on the edge of your seat watching *Oyster Mushroom Growing*. Into crafts? Follow the steps for making paper from mushroom conk. Or join Larry on a mushroom hunt—one of the events on the site's calendar.

Once a year Larry and friends gear up for a Missoula landmark, the International Wildlife Film Festival, dusting off the mushroom costumes that have been stored in the rafters of his garage. For the parade that kicks off the event, one cohort wears a morel outfit, another is dressed as a chanterelle, and one as the poisonous amanita, carrying a sign that reads PICK YOUR FRIENDS CAREFULLY.

Larry says, "It's all connected: forests to morels, fires to morels, temperatures to morels, moisture to morels." Through Cold Mountain, Cold Rivers—a nonprofit environmental group—Larry works to spread the connection of land and people, if not to preserve mushrooms, to protect our forests. Larry knows where to look for morels and works with the Forest Service to help brace against as many as fifty thousand annual pickers who arrive to comb western forests.

After a hard day of hunting mushrooms, Larry likes to kick back and relax, but he passes by the bars with WELCOME HUNTERS posted over the door and instead pops in a CD—coincidentally one he coproduced: *Fungal Boogie*—and downs a batch of butter-fried grays. Hardly ZZ Top or Black Sabbath, it's a mixture of musical styles and lyrics, "Naematoloma" (named after a mushroom genus) one of his favorites. Mycological euphoria to be sure. ✦

The pregnant cow was stretched between two pickup trucks, headlights on, in an early spring snowstorm as cold but capable hands grabbed a scalpel and began the cesarean delivery. Ranch hands stood by, ready to pour hot water over the sutures to keep them from breaking. Not exactly a Hallmark moment but also not unusual for Orley Arthur, a large-animal veterinarian from Roundup.

Since the early 1950s, he's treated everything from lizards to tortoises to eagles, but the majority of his time is spent at clients' ranches, although he's quick to point out that they're not just clients but friends. "Old-timers ask you to stay for dinner; if you get there late, they ask you to stay the night." He grew up on a ranch, and even though he started out to be a lawyer decided he didn't want to work inside at a desk. "I wanted to improve the profitability of ranchers."

VETERINARIAN

ORLEY ARTHUR, ROUNDUP

Some are real characters, like the bow-legged, long-nosed, hard-eyed Sonny. "He had a PhD in profanity," Orley laughs. "Those old cowboys see things differently—they're not dumb, in fact they're rather smart. They just approach problems their own way." Driving home his point, he mentions one rancher who roped a bear, then put it in the barn with the cows, "But scared cows—and they were—won't give milk, so he grudgingly took the bear back to the woods."

Sometimes just getting to his patients is an experience. Once he stopped his truck on a gumbo road to get out and open a gate. Turning back, he found the truck had slid off the road, and even with chains on all four wheels, Montana's notorious gumbo (mud) had him. Winter's no better. "Once on a call up Cat Creek I was out in minus-thirty-five-degree temps and had to be picked up on a snowmobile to be taken the rest of the way."

The IRS didn't believe Orley's claim of 100,000 miles a year as an expense until his accountant showed up at the audit with a state map. Pointing out Orley's territory—from Lavina to Jordan—finally convinced them. Good thing they didn't press him for details on his income, which has included gallons of homemade wine, a rifle, and a huge slab of bacon that took two men to haul.

Not all his work takes him on the road. He's unfazed when a customer arrives with a yearling steer in the back of a sedan but still shakes his head at the two cowboys who showed up with a bull that had forced its head through the back truck window into the cab with them. During calving season as many as eight pickups have been lined up outside his shop waiting for C-sections. "It's more practical than me spending valuable time running out to each ranch. And I have a sterile environment here."

His primary focus is good nutrition, so he was understandably stumped when cattle he was treating for copper deficiency—a not uncommon condition—died. Looking deeper, Orley discovered that their drinking water was alkaline, which negated the treatment. "I like figuring out these kinds of mysteries because then I can apply them to other ranchers' situations," says Orley, who has developed a reputation as a bulldog at problem solving.

Without hesitation he says the worst case he ever treated was vibriosis, a bacterial disease that causes cattle to abort. By developing a vaccination program, Orley eliminated the bug that could have passed from ranch to ranch. At another spread he correctly identified bluetongue after others thought it was foot-and-mouth disease. "It's so rare I called out the feds to see it."

Although he enjoys sleuthing, a lot of his time is hands-on grunt work, whether setting a cow's broken leg or mending an injured deer. Pulling out a dead undelivered calf with a tractor sounds ghastly, but he notes, "Every large-animal vet in the state has this story—it's almost routine."

However, Orley learned that routine can become anything but, after responding to a horse caught in a cattle guard with a badly scraped leg. He dressed its wounds and released the animal, then discovered it had been bitten by a rabid skunk that was actually chewing on the scraped leg. All who came in contact with the horse had to be vaccinated for rabies. The horse died four months later.

You wouldn't think so but pregnancy-testing time can be a real knee-slapper—at least for the ranchers. To break up the monotony of running cow after cow through chutes to be tested, "ranch hands will slip in a steer with the females just to trip me up." Orley stays calm and with a barely a side glance tells them, "Steers are usually dry."

He's never been seriously injured—no major kicks or gores, just glancing blows—and attributes this good fortune to the fact that he grew up around animals: "I know how to read them." Bison, though, are a different story. They're remarkably fast, strangely enough because of their large windpipes, which give them more air and allow them to run faster than a horse. "When you hear a buffalo grunt, you should have already jumped the fence."

Old-time ranching is giving way to technology. Orley works with artificial insemination (AI) but now a computer tells him what kind of semen to use. Extracting the semen is also done electronically, although still very carefully. And no longer does he need to stick his whole arm in a cow's rectum to determine pregnancy—it's done through ultrasound. On the downside, ranches are being bought out by conglomerates, and instead of working with the owners, he's forced to deal with managers who want to operate by the numbers.

Even so, he encourages others to follow in his footsteps, but warns that you have to have a sense of humor to be a vet and deal often literally with a lot of "feces *bovus masculinus,* so you better watch where you step." ◆

The story goes that a fellow fed up with Montana winters left the state, heading south, snow shovel in hand. He said when he got far enough south to where someone had to ask him what he was carrying, that's where he'd live. That guy wasn't Paul Bronson. Paul thrives on snow and up until his retirement to Anaconda made his living off the white stuff.

Throughout his career Paul has had highs and lows, from 4,200 feet underground in the Kelly Mine to plowing out the 10,947-foot pass at the top of the Beartooth Highway. In between you could find him in the Berkeley Pit, behind the wheel of a big rig, on a small ranch in Charlo, and as maintenance chief and road superintendent in Billings. In summer and the shoulder seasons his focus was on maintaining 3,200 lane miles of road and inspecting and repairing 520 bridges, the biggest obstacle being caravans of tourist-toting RVs. But come winter his attention turned to bigger things: snowplows.

A snowplow operator's job can be thankless as well as dangerous. Every year at least four trucks have been rear-ended, sometimes by semis. Paul says of his eighty-five-man crew, "They're working in the most hazardous conditions to help people who shouldn't be out in that weather, clearing roads and spreading salt and aggregate." As motorists we tend to forget about the good they do and instead blame them for the fateful pebble that just left a nice star pattern on our pristine windshield. There's some consolation in knowing that the people we hold responsible aren't immune to chips and cracks. Paul says, "We have cars too and get them the same as everyone else."

While the rest of us are mowing our lawns in June, road crews attend snow conferences like the one sponsored by the Pacific Northwest Snow

---

BEARTOOTH HIGHWAY SUPERVISOR

PAUL BRONSON, ANACONDA

Fighters. As always the hot topic is researching the best materials for snowy roads—safety being the main concern. Montana uses 100,000 tons of salt in a season, most of it in late fall and early spring when snow is heaviest and roads are at their worst. "We have to use salt, even though it's expensive, because it melts into the snowpack and keeps a hold on the aggregate. Without it aggregate is too fine and blows away." But salt attracts wildlife, creating yet another road hazard, so they're switching over to deicers.

Come spring, without a doubt the most challenging stretch of road is the Beartooth Highway. Charles Kurault touted it as the most beautiful highway in America—then again he never had to plow it open. As maintenance chief Paul and his crew would spend at least six weeks to get it tourist-ready for the Friday before Memorial Day weekend. Opening this lifeline between Red Lodge and Cooke City is a political hot button—seasonal incomes depend on it. Despite all the

work, Nature has the final say, and there isn't a month that snow doesn't bring out the plows, often closing the road. If snow isn't the culprit, Paul also has to deal with boulders, trees, and avalanches, all of which can knock out guardrails (the last thing you want on this highway), or poor visibility that closes the road. "But it's all part of opening the Beartooth," he says.

The Beartooth Highway is not for the acrophobe. Even the stoutest driver may have a moment of doubt negotiating hairpin turns that drop off into Red Lodge. Paul says that even in good weather at least a couple vehicles catch fire each year from overheating on their way up the mountain. The hazardous curves force people to drive extra carefully, motor homes especially, so accidents, although they do happen, are rare. Every year some semis ignore the signs about no truck traffic and violate the barricade, only to find themselves stuck and unable to turn around. Some have abandoned their rigs, and Paul's crew had to drive them back out.

Driving the highway in summer, with not a flake in sight, you can't miss seeing the snow poles along the edge of the road. Try to imagine plowing in the worst weather following nothing more than these skinny sticks. At one bad spot known as the Line Drift, snow was 42 feet deep one year, and Paul called in a bulldozer that had to begin its work more than four stories above the roadway. "With that much snow the poles are useless, but the snowplow operators know the road like the back of their hand"—they'd better. The resulting 40-foot-high canyon of snow, just wide enough for one car, made the evening news.

In a typical winter Paul deploys an armada of equipment to clear the Beartooth: V-plows punch through drifts, blade plows push it off to the side, and snowblowers spit out 400 tons of winter wonderland an hour. Warm spring snows are tough, and crews work at night so the heavy snow doesn't clog the equipment, but Paul remembers one winter when they had to bring out the heavy artillery—dynamite.

In this environmental tundra, ironically global warming creates a whole new set of problems for road crews. Subterranean ice glaciers have melted during warmer years, causing the road to settle and sink, each year getting worse. Just 20 feet below the surface, drillers have hit 40 feet of ice; plans are in the works to build bridges to span it.

The chasm cut through the pass each May reveals a layered history of last winter's storms in the wall the plows leave behind. However, most folks don't care about the work that went into creating their canvas—they're here to scratch their names in the snow; one enterprising artist carved out an entire mural.

These days Paul's biggest challenge is clearing his driveway, and although he no longer has a crew to help, he's not about to pick up his shovel and head south. ✦

The setting could be out of a Zane Grey western: Charlie Russell country, deceptively flat at first glance, with coulees and draws that break at the Missouri River. A gravel road in serious need of switchbacks plunges 800 feet from the prairie to the river. The Missouri flows past swiftly but strangely silent; only an occasional ripple betrays its presence. Four bighorn sheep cross the road to drink as a car approaches the riverbank. With a jarring blare of the car horn, the sheep scatter and Susan Sanford comes to life on the other side, running barefoot, always barefoot, down the hill from the mobile home headquarters to pick up her fare.

The McClelland/Stafford ferry is one of three in Montana. Its operators are paid by Blaine County, wages ironically coming out of the bridge fund, which is still more cost-effective than installing a bridge. Traffic isn't heavy, although there are regulars with ranchland on both sides. Susan says, "There's a bridge 10 miles upriver but it's a circuitous route, and the ferry saves a lot of time." She explains the confusing name: "Coming from the north it's the McClelland, from the south it's the Stafford. It was named after men on opposite sides of the river."

FERRY OPERATOR

SUSAN SANFORD, McCLELLAND

Susan was born on a ranch about 6 miles north as the crow flies—"really on the ranch, not in a hospital," she says. After graduating from high school as an honor student, she took computer classes in college but decided that "making big bucks at an inside job wouldn't make me happy, so I quit." Later she took an auto body course, where she painted her pickup—"I got an A, the best grade, even better than the guys. I wouldn't say that I quit college; I'll most likely take courses on and off throughout my life like my mother did."

But all along the way she had company, and it nearly killed her: "I spent eight hard years as an alcoholic," beginning when she was fifteen. She landed in an abusive marriage, divorced, then worked "at a bar of all places, meeting all the wrong people and doing all the wrong things." She was living off a sack of potatoes when her mother suggested she come back and work at the ferry. But that didn't stop her drinking; she'd down a case of beer a day, often beginning early in the morning. Susan's alcoholism led to violent tendencies, and a judge eventually sentenced her to counseling and rehab. "I went to spin dry, as I call it, and have been sober ever since. Quitting has completely changed my life."

To outsiders, Susan's ferry life appears isolated; the setting certainly is, but there's plenty to keep her busy. Operating only in summer means ferrying regulars as well as tourists, sometimes as many as several dozen lined up waiting for the two-minute ride. Susan has noticed an increase in river traffic "probably because of the Lewis and Clark bicentennial," and they come from all over the world. "We should have one of those big maps so travelers can put a pushpin in to identify their hometowns." She recalls one of the Missouri's more unusual, almost surreal, scenes, when she transported a group from India, "with turbans."

One summer Susan helped a group from the University of Calgary do a study along the Missouri and Milk Rivers on the western small-footed bat. Her excitement is uncontained: "We were out there with flashlights, catching and studying them—it was great!" Not so great are the critters she shoos from her garden: "There are lots of snakes hanging around there—mostly bull, blue racers, and garters," but one very hot, dry summer she had to remove three rattlesnakes from the yard, too.

Tuesdays are generally slow, but Wednesday is grocery day, entailing a trip to Lewistown, 60 miles one way. Although Winifred is much closer, it's more efficient to do the weekly run. It's usually Susan's job to go because if the truck breaks down, she can fix it. The gravel road to Lewistown is a superhighway compared to the road north of the ferry; it's bentonite, aka gumbo, and "gets like a bar of soap in the slightest drizzle. I had a four-wheeler stuck at least twice."

Her mother, Grace, is the main person at the ferry and runs most of the trips. Besides filling in for Mom, Susan's a jack-of-all-trades: She keeps the gas tank filled in the ferry's tractor motor, greases the cables, deals with a cantankerous pickup, and sews—she's made the gown for her Old West–themed wedding. In her spare time she tends the garden, deals with antiquated plumbing, and gets in a little fishing and swimming. Their trailer is temporary housing, and each fall the pipes need to be drained and the whole place shut down. She packs up the menagerie of dog, cat, and birds, named simply Dog, Kitty, and Bird, and then heads inland for the winter.

During several off-seasons, Susan wasn't far from the water; in fact, she was in it. Decked out in bikini top and flipper legs, she worked as a mermaid at the Sip-N-Dip—a funky tiki-style bar—in Great Falls, where customers would tape tips to the viewing window behind the bar. The bottom of the pool was the ceiling of an underground parking garage and the water was cold in winter, so bad that an ear infection caused bleeding and hearing loss.

The ferry has been there as long as Susan can remember. "I think that as long as people are interested in its novelty, and preserving the historic, nostalgic, and romantic quality, it will stay in use." The only thing that has hampered its performance has been bad gas.

A pickup sits on the southern bank, one of the regulars who doesn't have to announce his presence. Grace is getting groceries, and Susan picks up her hat as she heads down the hill to ferry the rancher across, Dog nipping at her bare heels. ✦

Al Grandchamp braids hackamores purely for the joy of making them. And he's made lots of them—hundreds, in fact. Yet he's only ever sold four—enough to make any modern-day marketer cringe. Al is a rawhider but obviously not a bottom-line kind of guy.

Rawhide is cowhide with the hair removed, and Al likes using it to make a hackamore, a bitless bridle used for leading a horse that's especially good for horse training. His creations take shape on a kitchen table in his log home. It's the same 135-year-old cabin that his pioneering grandparents built—the place where his mother was born. The house is freshly painted, contrasting sharply with the rugged dirt street out front that seems to have changed so little. This is Radersburg, set in the foothills of the Elkhorn Mountains, where the pavement ends but not the history.

Born in Heron in 1907, Al has plenty of history to share. He grew up in the lumberjack

RAWHIDER

AL GRANDCHAMP, RADERSBURG

country of Thompson Falls but looked forward to spending summers with relatives in Radersburg, where he was introduced to the Riverside Ranch, one of the biggest cattle ranches around. Like any youngster, he was eager to learn to ride a horse and work the cattle, and the ranch hands were just as eager to oblige him. He hung out with them daily, helping out at the cow camps in the mountains. At the ranch Al paraded horses for prospective buyers who arrived by train from Helena. It was here that he learned firsthand the finer points of horsemanship—something that's been a constant in his life.

A few years later while on a pack trip in the backcountry of Idaho with Charles Williamson, a veterinarian and the author of *Breaking and Training the Stock Horse,* Al met Lige Lewis, a braider from Boise. He, more than anyone, told Al about braiding rawhide and encouraged him to pursue it. This craft was a perfect match with Al's interest in horse training. Believing that if you want something done right, it's best to do it yourself, years later Al began producing hackamores that outperformed any others.

As a working adult, Al spent much of his time teaching English, first in Ronan, where he met his wife, Nea, then in Simms, and later in Livingston, eventually becoming superintendent at Columbia Falls. But in between he ranched. "I went wherever the best money was at the time," he says. The braiding skills he learned as a youth were put aside until he was in his forties, not unusual for this man, who took up team roping when he was in his sixties.

"Hands-on braiding gives you an appreciation for the workmanship of others," notes Al, and he can tell a lot from a hackamore. "There are some fine braiders out there—better than me," he says, "but I understand horses—I train horses, and I know how to create the proper balance and proportion so the hackamore works right. It can't just look nice." Up until just a few years ago, Al passed

on the braiding basics to people who attended his horsemanship clinics held throughout the West and Canada. Although he's made a riding crop or two, his specialty remains hackamores.

The rawhide Al uses is the same material dog chews are made from, but he starts with strips. "I used to make my own but it was quite a process. First you have to soak the hide until it's flexible, then wrap it in cloth and put the whole thing in a plastic bag to temper it until it's ready to cut. I now buy precut rawhide." After weaving, the strips dry rock hard but are susceptible to rain, which can do in a hackamore, making it soggy. Rawhide is difficult to work and there's a lot of waste; leather, however, is a different matter. Al still cuts his own leather strips and in fact had a friend make him a special machine-tooled jig, a real time-saver. His hands are steady as he shows how to put a bevel on the leather strips. In contrast he demonstrates the cow camp method range hands use to make their own strips with a board, a bent horseshoe nail, and a very sharp pocketknife. As he deftly bevels the edges, you get the feeling he's made more than his share around a campfire out on the range. Although he patiently teaches others his craft, they often lose interest when they find out how long the process takes—about six hours for Al to produce a finished hackamore.

Surprisingly, it all begins with a piece of rope. Al prefers used team rope because it's slightly more flexible, and the ropers just throw it away, opting for new gear instead. He braids an 8-inch band, the nosepiece, on a straight piece of rope, then forms it into a teardrop shape, large enough to fit over a horse's muzzle. The ends are then joined with a heel, or pineapple, knot, which he feels is the most important part of a good hackamore. "The weight of the heel knot and the placement of the side 'buttons' dictate how well it works."

Every craft has its master, and Luis Ortega is often considered to be the greatest hackamore maker. A top-quality show piece can fetch up to $1,000—these usually are very decorative and colorful. Al's, on the other hand, are functional, and of the more than two hundred he's made, he's traded with friends or given away nearly all of them.

For fifty years Al's been weaving and creating and handing out hackamores, but he's slowed down some because his hands have become stiff. Still, in nice weather you can find this gentle man working in one of his outbuildings on an occasional project. A dog barks in the distance, a pickup cruises by leaving swirls of dust in its wake, and Al glances up from his work to nod a greeting. Radersburg hasn't changed much. ◆

When Montana's speed limit was "reasonable and prudent," it was easy to zip past Forsyth and overlook the three-story structure topped with huge red block letters visible from the interstate. Now that traffic crawls by at 75 miles an hour, drivers might ease off the gas long enough to wonder about the 8-foot-tall words HOTEL HOWDY on the downtown building's roof. If they took the time to actually stop in, they might run into Esther Dean, who could tell them everything they'd ever want to know about the place. "The Howdy has been around for one hundred years without ever closing," she says, "not even during the Depression." Esther's more than a local historian; she's the granddaughter-in-law of its builder, wife of the former owner, and mother of the present owner.

But to know the Hotel Howdy, you first need to know Esther. An only child of a district judge, she was brought up in a loving, close-knit

HOTEL HOWDY HISTORIAN

ESTHER DEAN, FORSYTH

family—she was cultured and well schooled, with a degree from Carleton College, the Harvard of the West. They rubbed elbows with the Rankins and Charlie Russell. She recalls telling her father later, "Why the heck didn't you get him to paint something?" Esther and her parents traveled all over the country by train, and she remembers being in New York City when "there was still ticker tape in the streets from Lindbergh's parade," something the average kid in Miles City only got to read about in the newspaper.

Perhaps it was because of this secure upbringing that she was attracted to the rakish Walter Dean. Also an only child, his family life hardly mirrored Esther's. He had an unloving upbringing and constantly sought security, which is probably why he returned to Forsyth after two years of world travel. His career in law was brief but long enough to meet Esther. He opened her eyes to a whole new world on their first date when he taught her how to shoot a pistol. "He told me how to squeeze, and I shot a light out," she laughs, "but he married me anyway. Ironically, he had a girlfriend at one time who was a redhead and later another girl named Esther. Then he met me—a redhead named Esther.

"Which brings us back to the Howdy," she says. "Walter's grandfather built it shortly after the turn of the century and called it the Commercial." His mother and aunt owned and operated the hotel, which became a center of commerce for rail-traveling merchants to stay and set up their displays on the mezzanine. Things went along fine but just about the time Walter took over, motels were popping up along the highway. The post–World War II economy began to take its toll, and the hotel struggled to keep up with the times.

Renovation began in the 1950s and hasn't stopped—the building is always in various stages of remodeling. The mezzanine, where Jeanette Rankin once announced she was running for Congress, was considered wasted space and con-

verted to apartments. The entire building was rewired—Esther still has the receipt: $130. Walter felt a new look deserved a new name, and "Howdy Hotel" was first suggested by his partner's girlfriend after her favorite greeting. But Walter had a cheap side; rather than pay ranchers for billboard space, he erected the now famous letters so they could be seen from the highway.

To entice patrons, he decided to add a bar and offer live music. "That would have shocked his teetotaling grandfather," Esther says. What's more, Walter convinced Esther that her skill in classical piano could be a fine complement to his jazz saxophone and clarinet. "I was trained in classical, not bar-type music," she says, still horrified at the thought. Yet each weekend, there they were, center stage—Walter laying down the rhythm, with Esther, raised on Bach, hammering out jazz on the keyboard. They became quite popular and stayed on the marquee well into the 1980s. Esther worked one month as the Howdy's desk clerk, but when Walter suggested they take over the hotel as a team, she replied, "Your mother died down there and I don't intend to."

Instead she became the town's librarian and immersed herself in local history. She says, "Grandpa Dean had a thing about photography [think of the fun he'd have today with a digital camera], snapping thousands of photos of Forsyth and surrounding areas, many of Colstrip as it was being developed." Esther had possession of them, but because one of her teenage sons smoked in the attic where they were stored, she feared for their safety and sent them off to the historical society in Helena, where they were declared the "best collection of photos of a small town in all of Montana." Esther was instrumental in writing and compiling the local history book, *They Came and Stayed,* issued for Montana's centennial. It couldn't have been done without her input, but through oversight, her name doesn't appear anywhere in the volume. She doesn't mind, preferring instead to stay out of the spotlight, although she was happy to accept when given a Citizen of the Year award sometime later.

Even with all of the Howdy's renovations, some things haven't changed much. Guests walk the same floors as their counterparts did nearly a century ago, and at $20 a night the rates are still the best around. Hunters stay here as well as travelers seeking a night of living history, and the railroad has a standing order for rooms for its workers. Despite the lack of vegetation to stop the wind in this prairie town, the HOTEL HOWDY letters have weathered and been refurbished but they've never blown down. But of course, some change is inevitable. The development of nearby Colstrip produced a whole new clientele. Spotlights make the rooftop letters visible at night. Walter has passed on. Esther isn't the physical presence she once was at the hotel, but she's still involved with the Howdy and other local history—it's her life. ◆

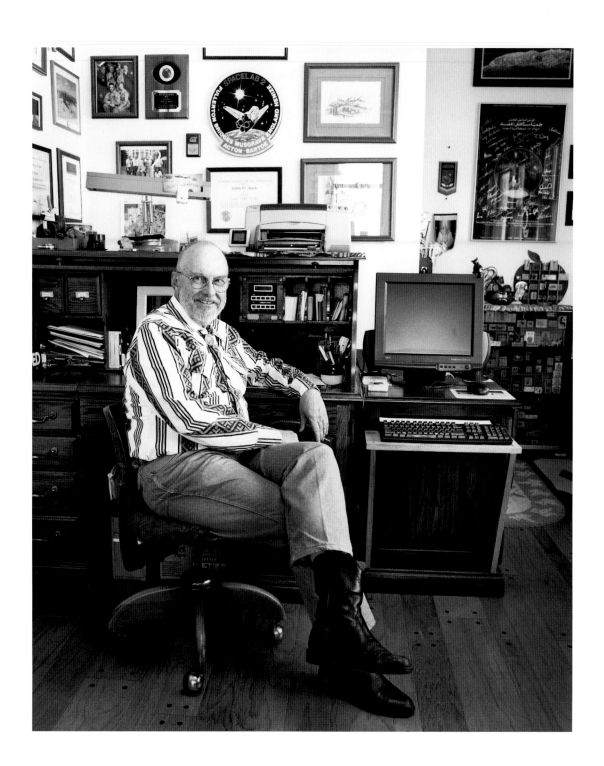

Big Sky country has a whole different meaning to Loren Acton, but that's because he's seen it like no other Montanan has: streaking around the earth at 18,000 miles an hour.

Growing up on a ranch just south of Lewistown in the 1940s, Loren didn't have aspirations to become an astronaut, let alone Montana's first. The distant youngest of five children, he spent a lot of time alone, reading mostly, not Buck Rogers or Flash Gordon but about real science and adventure, which he found far more entertaining.

When he entered Montana State University, it was his brother who suggested he major in physics. "His advice was pivotal in my life but I was scared to death of flunking out." He got his doctorate in solar physics, "essentially, science of the sun," he says, which led to further study in astrogeophysics and eventually his seat on a space shuttle. "Talk about irony: *Astronaut* wasn't even in

ASTRONAUT

LOREN ACTON, BOZEMAN

the dictionary my wife gave me when I was in college."

Although science came naturally to Loren, his color blindness made some things, like mineral identification, downright tough. But armed with his degree, he made another major decision and applied for a $4,000 fellowship to study upper atmospheric physics even though he didn't know enough about it to fill out the application form. An intense seminar got him the grant, and soon Loren was working with a navy crew to put a solar satellite into space. At the time, satellites were in their infancy and Loren's first launch crash-landed in Cuba. The second attempt did no better, ending up in the Pacific Ocean.

In California he joined researchers at Lockheed, who were developing experiments to be conducted in space. They decided someone from the company should be on the mission to oversee the work—a payload specialist. "I jumped at the chance to write up the job description and made sure color blindness wasn't an obstacle." Not coincidentally, Loren perfectly fit the description of the ideal candidate and became Lockheed's first astronaut as well as one of the first scientists selected for a shuttle mission.

The countdown went smoothly until T minus three seconds, when the main engines shut down and they had to abort. Seventeen days later they were back on board, this time with liftoff after a four-hour delay due to weather in Spain. But five minutes up, one of the three engines shut down and they had to dump fuel to lighten the craft so the remaining engines could get them into orbit. Surprisingly, safety wasn't Loren's main concern. "I worried they would abort the flight and I'd never get into space," he says. In 1985, after seven years of delays, the mission was in orbit, and Loren knew it: About ninety seconds later he became ill. "It's called SAS," he says, "space adaptation syndrome. I had it for four days; it sure put my ego in its place."

The next eight days were filled with scientific experiments, but there was always time for sightseeing. "The view is just like you see in pictures, only better. It's really obvious by city lights that most of our population lives along the coasts." He watched magnificent auroras and marveled at the planet's airglow but more than anything was impressed by lightning storms that lit up cloud banks. "Spectacular!"

The last frontier isn't for the claustrophobe, but being confined in a room the size of a camper didn't faze Loren. "In weightlessness you get to use all the volume. It only bothered me when I put on the flight helmet and had to breathe through a hose." SpaceLab 2's meals made airline food look gourmet: freeze-dried and the water laced with iodine; his six-cup-a-day coffee habit quickly turned to fruit juice to mask the taste. Although space itself is quiet, inside the craft it was anything but: Fans and pumps that keep the environment going are noisy, but "sleep was never a problem—I was dead tired."

It doesn't take a rocket scientist to know that what goes up must come down, but the automated process of slowing the craft and rotating it for reentry didn't go as planned. It had to be done manually and "even though I had complete faith in our captain," their fuel was redlined (they were low) because of the dump on takeoff. "Other than that, reentry was as exciting as watching grass grow." Because he didn't have a window seat, he played gravity games, releasing a wad of paper to see how quickly it would drop as they left orbit, and did leg exercises to prepare for walking on terra firma again. Landing was smoother than a commercial airliner.

He would have flown again but the program was canceled after the *Challenger* disaster. Like most Americans, he clearly remembers where he was that day—onstage lecturing to high school students in Worland, Wyoming. Loren was immediately approached by news media, who "came to me because I was a civilian and could talk about it; government employees couldn't. It was a tough day." Although he has retired several times—"My interests are a mile wide and a micron deep"—he still goes to work at MSU to input and organize data, and through his own grants, he does research on a telescope that photographs the sun's corona.

As a kid Loren never imagined that he'd go from riding his pony to a one-room schoolhouse to circling the earth at 5 miles per second, from 190 miles up. But knowing what his father experienced puts it all in perspective for him: He was born fifteen years before the flight at Kitty Hawk but lived to see his son fly in space. An astronaut is defined as someone who's flown beyond the earth's atmosphere, and that would be Loren. "I remember looking out the window of the space shuttle," he recalls, "and thinking to myself, who'd have ever expected a country boy from Fergus County, Montana, to end up here?" ◆

Rob Fraser's childhood dream wasn't typical of a boy growing up in Boston or Seattle or any metropolitan area, but in Montana it never raised an eyebrow. "I always wanted to be an auctioneer and own a livestock auction—the whole operation," he says. His family raised Herefords and sold them through sales on their ranch, where "five hundred people would show up; it was quite a social event." When Rob was five years old, his family would drop him off at the cattle auction in Billings: "I loved the people there. I was fascinated by the auctioneers."

You don't just wake up one day and begin selling cattle. Rob started out small, real small, with a pie sale at the Congregational church in Big Timber. "At auction school you don't really learn the trade—just how poor you are," he laughs. Like most, he says, "I started out by doing freebies—selling junk and books, then antiques and cars." In Montana you don't need to be licensed or bonded,

LIVESTOCK AUCTIONEER

ROB FRASER, MILES CITY

but at one of his first sales, in California, that wasn't the case. "I wasn't bonded there and had a sale shut down when I was only one hour into it."

While working on his dream, he was also working at a ranch supply store, where a sales rep for KBIT radio approached him. Rob said he'd consider advertising if they had ag-related programming, but they didn't. So they suggested he do it. "Not only did I have the program, I *was* the program—two five-minute spots a day."

Although radio stardom wasn't what he wanted, it paid off later when he started his own company: "It looked real nice on my resume. It opened a lot of doors."

Through hard work, a business degree, a little luck, and a sense of humor, he's now the co-owner and main mouthpiece of Miles City Livestock Commission Company, which when he bought it in 1995 was selling 19,000 cattle a year; it's now turning over 100,000. "It's not about selling, though, it's about psychology and excitement," he says. Every Tuesday he bangs his gavel, sending buyers and sellers home with prize stock, a far cry from when he had to go door-to-door to find something to sell. "It was a catch-22. I couldn't sell cattle without buyers and couldn't get buyers without cattle."

Miles City Live, a huge complex on the west edge of town, employs forty-eight people, at least a fourth of them women, Rob's favorite workers. "They're tireless and reliable," and he's not saying that just because his wife is nearby. He's head over heels for Cindy and gives her a lot of credit in the operation. "She handles the finances," he says, then grins: "Besides, she even smells good."

In 2002 his business took the next step, forming frontierstockyards.com, an online auction. "The ag business is very tech oriented, and our first Internet sale went over big. Buyers often still call to bid, "but you can hear them on their computers in the background. Forty-three percent of our sales are through the keyboard." As a result,

four times a year 20,000 head of Montana and Wyoming cattle are sold to bidders from Philadelphia to Australia, sitting in their homes while viewing cattle or an occasional ostrich, llama, or emu on a computer screen. Rob likes the arrangement because of lower overhead, but he still gets only a very small percentage of the gross sale.

In eastern Montana all roads lead to Miles City, or at least they did in the late 1800s when cattle trails hooked up with the railroad. But it happens again on the third weekend each May, when I–94 does a bang-up business for four or five days, as mobs descend on this cow town for its famous Bucking Horse Sale. The tradition started in 1950 when an auctioneer with a bunch of wild horses paid riders to buck them for potential buyers—he got quite a crowd. Rob says that changes in professional rodeos have had an impact on the horse sale. "It's become a serious sport, and the larger ones have turned to producing their own bucking horses, but some still need a sale like ours." One thing that hasn't changed is that the auction is always outdoors and it's rained at least one day each year, ever since Rob can remember.

"Cowboy Mardi Gras" has become less about the horse sale and more about partying, but there's still a lot of interest in seeing grown men thrown to the ground. So in the name of civic duty, Rob puts aside thoughts of his own business, dons his auctioneer hat, and makes sure that each horse gets ridden, although by the end of the auction it's not unusual to run short of riders. One night, after the crowd had thinned out, only one fellow—a former Canadian saddle bronc champ— agreed to get on the final horse, after a group anted up $500. He warbled the Canadian national anthem while having an incredible ride before being catapulted off, and "amazingly landed firmly on his feet, only to stumble and fall into a mud puddle," Rob laughs. At a local bar he shared his wealth "on anyone who needs a drink." It was gone in twenty minutes.

Montana and surrounding states are the main source for bucking horses, and quite a few come from Alberta, but "it's been a growing problem getting them across the border." Surprisingly many of the buyers come from New York and New Jersey and think nothing of dropping close to $5,000 for a good bucker. Rob says that one sold for a whopping $12,000.

Even when Rob's not working, he's not far from horses, teaching his daughter competitive riding. "She's a fifth-generation Montanan and really proud of it." He is, too, and points to his belt buckle with the family's Walking Canes brand. Rob no longer has to go door-to-door in search of cattle, but still does freebies, like 4-H auctions— only now it's because he wants to. ◆

Americans have taken to comfort food. Mom's meat loaf, macaroni and cheese, and pot roast remind us of home, of better days perhaps. But if you have Nordic blood in your veins, nothing says lovin' like lutefisk. Its name alone conjures up a warm fishy smell, and it's a rare Scandinavian who could resist plates of the mysterious pale gelatinous substance bathed in oceans of melted butter and cream sauce. In northwestern Montana, one man in particular stands out as the king of cod: Dan Howard.

This Libby native works for the Forest Service, specializing in silviculture, planting and thinning trees. So how do twenty-five years of dealing with trees prepare Dan for making this delicacy? They don't. He's a member of the Sons of Norway, known for their lutefisk dinners, and the chief cook. Dan says, "Our dinners aren't open to the public the way they used to be because the lutefisk is so expensive. To throw a dinner anymore,

LUTEFISK MAKER

DAN HOWARD, LIBBY

it's more a labor of love—we barely break even."

Dan's been a member of the Sons for more than thirty years, getting his exposure to making lutefisk when he was in his early twenties. At one dinner some of the older members had him observe the cooking process, telling him that someday he would be the one to take over. Those elders have passed on, and today Dan's the top dog, proud to be carrying on the tradition and knowing he's doing it right.

The Sons of Norway, originally formed in the United States as an insurance group, developed into an international organization that now includes women. When Dan joined it was a very social thing, but he notes that "times have changed and like so many fraternal organizations these days, it's getting tough to recruit younger members." His lodge has about ninety Sons, some of whom are more active than others. "A few come only for the lutefisk dinners."

Lutefisk is as Scandinavian as lefse (crepe) and traditionally served on Christmas Eve. But just because your father's a Viking doesn't mean you get all warm and mushy at the thought of the stuff. Dan says, "I hated it as a kid. It stank. I think they process it differently to remove the odor, and now I like it." Lutefisk (literally translated, "lye fish") has gotten a bad reputation, but if it's cooked properly and doused in butter, it can taste like lobster. No self-respecting lodge would be without a lutefisk dinner, but once a year is enough because it takes lots of preparation and money to do it up right. "Some people bake it, but we don't. Tradition calls for boiling—if you want baked fish, go to a restaurant," says Dan.

Cod doesn't come out of the ocean as lutefisk. Distributors preserve and treat it until it's pure white. Dan notes, "Most places won't tell you how it's done—that's their trade secret," but he gladly shares the cooking process, which is almost a celebration in itself.

It begins when Dan and about three or four others cut open the bags of fish, prepare the cheesecloth, and lay in beverages of choice for the workers. It takes about three days to prepare and thaw the fish, almost always with a lot of joking and of course plenty of liquid refreshment.

But Dan insists that it's serious business, and if you want dinner on Saturday, you better begin thawing on Wednesday. Lye, not something you would ordinarily eat, is used as a preservative and actually lends the fish its flavor, but through a series of water changes, it's carefully removed. Then of course the fish needs to be cooked. Two pots of salted water are kept boiling, and chunks of lutefisk wrapped in cheesecloth are first dropped into one pot to preheat them, then into the second to finish them off. "If it's done right, it flakes. Lutefisk that's gooey or sloppy is overcooked," Dan warns.

Libby doesn't have the corner on lutefisk—there are pockets of Scandinavians all over Montana, and come fall it's not too difficult to find your own stash of fish. A typical "lutefeast" anywhere in the state includes the famous fish, mashed or boiled potatoes, veggies, lefse, and some sort of dessert. And for the cod-fearing few, some dinners also offer Swedish meatballs. In Libby it's a little different. "The dinners are now for members only," Dan says, "sort of a reward for those who have worked diligently throughout the year on other lodge activities such as preparing for the Nordicfest or working on our float."

The Nordicfest—an annual Libby highlight—was started in 1985 as a way to bring people to town and boost the economy. The village's brown tones and weathered wood gave way to festive colors and decorative Nordic motifs. During the second week of September, the population swells and the Sons of Norway get dressed up in full regalia, complete with helmets. Lodge members who aren't whooping it up on their float are manning their booth and dishing out lefse, "Vikings on a stick" (spicy deep-fried lean ground

meat), and rosettes (fried pastries). For Dan and his group, Nordicfest is not just a four-day fling—cooking and freezing begins in January.

But it's not all work, and Dan says that they don't mind poking a little fun at themselves. He points to a bumper sticker that reads, "When lutefisk is outlawed, only outlaws will have lutefisk." Or the festival button: "Lutefisk: the piece of cod that passes all understanding," a play on words in a Lutheran church service. And humor isn't limited to the United States. "There are groups in Norway who don cowboy hats and have American instead of lutefisk dinners," he says.

Dan shares a Nordic knee-slapper: "How do you get rid of a skunk under your porch? You throw lutefisk under there. Then the problem is, how do you get rid of the Norwegians under your porch?"

Uff da—what a cod. ◆

Friends call her "Half Off" because they think "I'm not serious about anything. I joke a lot." When Annette Linder talks about her quilts and family—often intertwining the two—she can be very serious. Her extended family of seven kids runs the gamut from toddler to college; nephews and grandchildren round out the group. In the center of Annette's living room is a quilting frame that takes up most of the floor space, and when she sits down to quilt, seating becomes a hot commodity. She has cleverly rigged the frame to pulleys that allow her to raise it to the ceiling. "That keeps it out of the way of sticky fingers," she says, "but I never see my light fixture."

Annette grew up with three sisters and five brothers. "We were all treated the same. Besides traditional chores, the boys cooked and cleaned and girls drove tractors and hauled hay." The older women taught her to sew, beginning on an old treadle machine—but instead of quilts she was turning out tents and tepees. Her parents organized powwows, from butchering beef to providing quilts, so "I was always sewing. I can't remember not quilting." She does recall that it wasn't until she was about twelve that her mother didn't rip the stitching out of one of Annette's creations.

QUILTER

ANNETTE LINDER, WOLF POINT

For twenty-five years before she set up shop at home, she worked in Poplar at Assiniboine and Sioux Tribal Industries (A&S)—with five hundred employees, the "biggest small business in the state." Here she sewed for the government: Camouflage netting, duck blinds, and oil spill nets were shipped out as fast as they left her needle. As jobs at A&S were cut, hers became more desk oriented. "Even though I enjoyed other parts of the job, I didn't want to be a receptionist, so I quit," taking with her years of sewing machine maintenance know-how, which came in handy when she began making quilts full-time. "I use different machines for different jobs," she explains, and has several set up at one time, but complains, "I've run through six machines in less than a year."

She's known in Wolf Point for her nimble thimble and is constantly bombarded with orders for quilts, nearly all of which are for ceremonial giveaways. At a giveaway someone is honored, usually a family member, but it can include graduation, weddings, or other landmark events. Giveaways at powwows can be huge, involving hundreds of quilts, so it's no surprise that Annette, a member of the Canoe Paddler and Red Bottom bands of the Assiniboine, gets orders from other tribes. Color preferences differ from tribe to tribe but she notes that some, such as the Cheyenne, will use any color except green. Quilts have replaced buffalo robes as the gift of choice, with the Sioux and Assiniboine becoming known for their star patterns.

Annette, however, has given some of her stars a different twist, incorporating bright colors on a black background. "I think this has been influenced by the Amish" who taught some natives to quilt, "but the Assiniboine don't usually use black." A customized, heavily detailed quilt can cost $1,000. Although most are half that, each one is sized for a double bed and sports western motifs and brilliant colors, some in satin, some in cotton—there's no limit to what she'll use.

Annette unfolds a quilt with a bronc rider in the center and says her most unusual request was of a dragon; also memorable is a bowlegged cowboy on a horse, but most tastes run toward the more common eagle and bear. Reservations don't have quilting bees as such, but local women rally when Annette needs them to fill a larger order or if she's creating a complex design. Precious spare time finds her haunting the Ben Franklin store in Wolf Point for fabric. Satin means a trip to Culbertson, and "people always drop off remnants when they come to visit."

Her house is full of material—and kids. The whole family pitches in to run the ranch, where they raise horses, cows, wheat, and hay. Even the smallest help feed the animals, turn on water—

the usual farm chores— but "at night we cut quilt fabric while listening to CDs of powwow music and sometimes dance Indian." Annette says, "I won't let the kids use rotary cutters; scissors do just fine." And while helping, they learn. "When I sew, even the youngest get exposed to counting, colors, and shapes. They learn to count because I need a certain number of pieces to complete a star pattern." Their reward is an education, but they make scrap quilts, too, that they sell for $75.

After the little ones are in bed for the night, Annette's serious side kicks in, and she puts her sewing machines through a grueling workout until well past 2:00 A.M. Then it's up at 6:30— "four hours of sleep at night suits me fine"—to tend to the crew, get the ranch work done, and quilt some more.

Annette's sewing talents don't stop at quilts. "I make bedspreads and Indian headdresses (wapesha) of porcupine and deer hair, and dancing dresses for powwows, for my kids and others." Annette encourages the children to sew their own dresses: "It keeps them from getting into trouble with drugs and booze and stuff." A jingle dress (jingles are made from Copenhagen chewing tobacco tin lids) will run its proud owner several hundred dollars, but there's no charge if the parents help. "I feel it's a way to create quality time for kids and parents working together."

Much of what Annette does is centered around children. For a Head Start Dental Fair she crafted a set of Bert and Ernie Indian hand puppets, but the hit of the fair was when she showed up in the crepe paper Big Bird costume she made. "It was hot and the suit curled," she laughs, lending some credence to her nickname. But there's nothing about her that's half off; Annette is right on. ✦

Montana is the victim of many misconceptions: Out-of-staters think we're snowed in year-round and that temperatures never climb above freezing. They're convinced we're overrun with cowboys and Indians, and many are unaware that we're the fly-fishing capital of the country. Mention that eastern Montana is known for its sugar beets and you may get a wink and a snide, "Sure it is," but not from Bill Michael; in fact, he'll give you a complete history of the sugar beet industry. He ought to know—he's been growing them for more than fifty years. He says proudly, "I've been around beets ever since I was six."

There's a reason Billings is sometimes called the Sugar City. "Eastern Montana's soil and climate are great for growing high-quality beets," says Bill. He explains that after an irrigation system was established in the late 1800s, city founders looked for a cash crop to take advantage of it—as it turned out, beets were perfect. But beet farming was backbreaking work, and realizing a large labor force was needed, civic leaders appealed to Eastern Europe for workers. The workers came, and what's more, they stayed—Bill's a third-generation beet grower.

SUGAR BEET GROWER

BILL MICHAEL, BILLINGS

He farms 410 acres passed down through his wife's family—in particular, her grandfather, a sheep rancher who became one of the wealthiest men in Montana. Sheep got Bill on his way, but "dogs from the subdivision attacked our flock so many times, we finally sold them," and beets became their main crop. "The standard of living was pretty low—we didn't even have electricity on the farm until 1941," he says.

In addition to growing the vegetables, Bill's an authority on the history of the Western Sugar Co-op. The company has undergone so many changes, it can be difficult to keep track of them all, but Bill can—he has a pile of neatly organized notes in front of him that he knows by heart. It was 1906 when the first crops were processed at the Billings Sugar Company, now the Western Sugar Co-op. In 1908 it merged with the granddaddy of sugar companies: Great Western Sugar. Things went along fine until a hostile takeover bankrupted them in 1969; later, growers tried to keep themselves in business by forming a co-op, but things went belly-up again in 1984. Bill notes, "We didn't grow beets that year. We grew a lot of corn instead, just to survive." The next year a British company bought the business but then tried to close it a few years later, so a fellow from Hardin put together a deal to buy the company. In 2000 a co-op was formed, representing three hundred members and comprising 128,000 acres.

Come April you'll find Bill out planting his land. "I used to have more but lost forty-two acres to the Yellowstone in just one year—one neighbor lost half his farm to the river." His seeds,

from the Beta Seed Company, have the unglamorous name of #8749. About the size of pencil erasers, "today's seeds are monogerms," Bill says. And that's a good thing. "They used to have multiple germs and produced more than one plant per seed, which meant time-consuming thinning. Russian scientists bred the monogerm, so there's no need to thin them anymore." Through breeding, beets have gotten lighter; what used to be a hefty five-pound veggie now comes in at about half that weight. But not even the best scientists have been able to make them resistant to insects and hailstorms, which reduce their sugar content by damaging the tops.

A sugar beet is shaped like a pink-and-white football with one end lopped off. That may seem obvious to some, but Bill chuckles as he recalls: "We had a bus group stop by. Later that evening at dinner they thanked us for a nice tour but remarked that they still didn't know what a sugar beet looked like. It never occurred to us that they hadn't seen one."

Harvesting has always been hard, hard work. On a typical October day, Bill is up at 5:30 A.M. heading out to dig beets that he'll store in piles. "Heat is our biggest worry; too much and they lose a lot of their sugar content." The laborious digging used to be done by hand with a machete-like knife known as the widow maker—it was easy to miss your mark and hit yourself. And that's in the field; even more dangerous was shoveling the final product, which flows like beach sand. The hapless shoveler was dangled like a spider over mounds of sugar in huge bins, with the hope that his harness wouldn't give out. Today farmers like Bill use automation, but it doesn't come cheap—a mechanical digger can run $70,000, but it can harvest six rows at a time with little threat to the operator.

For the beets it's a one-way truck ride to the co-op, some coming from as far as 150 miles. Unlike cane grown in a field, beets are harvested from the ground and must be thoroughly washed before they're processed. Slicing them into thin chips exposes more surface area, which yields more sugar. Bill explains the process in a nutshell: "The chips go through a series of machines that extract the juice, concentrate it, and eventually bag it as sugar. If the bag on your shelf is from sugarcane, it has to say so; if not, it's from beets, and you'd never be able to tell the difference. Chemically they're the same." The pulp that remains is compressed into pellets for animal feed.

Like any farmer in Big Sky Country, Bill's always gambling: against the economy, supply and demand (some manufacturers are turning to corn-based sweeteners), and of course, the weather. The processor usually has a huge inventory of perishable product, but the farmer doesn't get final payment until the following year—a long time to have to rob Peter to pay Paul. But as long as he's able and conditions are right, come spring Bill will plant Beta #8749 and cross his fingers. ◆

He's in the arctic, hundreds of miles from nowhere, in subzero temperatures, fighting against swirling, blinding snow, not another human being around—and he's having the time of his life. This is Doug Swingley on a good day, running the Iditarod, the World Series of sled dog racing. In addition to civilization, he's left behind 200,000 well-wishers in Anchorage at the start line, to be greeted by about 15,000 diehards in Nome just a little more than nine days and 1,167 miles later.

Doug has set Iditarod records, as well as broken his own; he's the oldest and the first non-Alaskan to win the race, and he's won it several times. Not too shabby for a former Stanford business graduate and hospital administrator, a job, he says, "I held for ten days before I decided sitting behind a desk wasn't for me." He chose instead to work as an estimator for a large construction company, in addition to running his ranch, and still found time to enter his first Iditarod in 1992.

What would possess a person to go to Alaska, in March no less, face sleep deprivation, get frostbitten, and run a pack of dogs in the dark? For anyone else it could be the $110,000 prize and a new pickup, but that's just icing on the cake for

SLED DOG RACER

DOUG SWINGLEY, LINCOLN

Doug. Like the skydiver, rock climber, or overpaid Green Bay Packer, he's hooked on the sport, falling in love with it when he and his brother Greg ran their first race, the John Beargrease in Minnesota. Pulled by six dogs from the animal shelter, they came in just three hours behind the world's best. "I said to my brother, 'Let's kick it up a notch and go for it with really good dogs.'" And they did, winning all the major races in the Lower 48, where his brother still holds most of the records.

Naturally, without good dogs there is no race. Doug, a fifth-generation Montanan, was raised on a ranch near Simms, but the farm dogs there were hardly race quality. Years later, when he moved to Lincoln, he started breeding his own. And like any great pursuit, feeding and taking care of dozens of dogs is expensive. "I was fortunate to get endorsements from a dog food company in just two years after starting out," he says. To Doug, training and raising the dogs is more fun than the racing itself. On his spread just outside of town, he has loads of house pets, but he's most proud of Elmer, patriarch of all his other dogs. The now retired husky was a two-time Golden Harness winner, an honor bestowed by the other racers on the best dog. But Elmer's the only sled dog to get his own room; the others are kept a quarter mile from the house "to avoid the stress of people."

As an excellent judge of animals, he says, "I've never raised a clunker." His puppies command about $700; better adults can fetch $20,000 to $30,000. And the money comes in handy: Although sponsors pick up the tab for dog food and his high-tech clothing, racing is incredibly expensive. His dogs go through twelve hundred

booties in a race (Doug stresses they're for wear and tear, not warmth); he doles out for vet bills, transportation, entry fees, lodging, equipment—plus there's the sled. Doug designs his own, preferring wood over the newer synthetics, then has it built by a man in Gallatin Gateway. "When wood breaks in racing, you can fix it yourself, like lacing on a willow branch to repair a runner."

Montana's winters are notorious, but even they couldn't prepare Doug for the 140-below-with-windchill conditions he experienced in one race. Training for the big event starts seriously in August, and it's not unusual to see Doug running the dogs in front of a wheeled sled before the snows come. "It's more about the dogs than anything—they're what's important. Each one has its own specialty. I'm merely the coach." He rotates about four or five from the team each year. "There's no lead dog—they're all lead dogs, but there is one that's key on each team."

Running the Alaskan wilderness at night is no problem for this hardy Montanan: "Nothing scares me." He does carry a weapon to protect his dogs from wolves and moose, but "they stay clear and don't bother us." The two thousand pounds of supplies he carted with him are sent out to various checkpoints, most of which are villages where mushers can ask for information about weather and terrain. Other than that, no assistance is allowed. There are strict rules regarding treatment of the dogs: They need to be allowed to sleep 50 percent of the time, more than the musher gets, not only because they're expensive but also because a musher's life can depend on them; thus no one ever questions or violates the animal rule.

Doug's celebrity status allows him the luxury of picking and choosing which races he'll enter, and he plans to compete as long as he's healthy. But fame has its price: Even without race travel he's home only three or four months of the year: "One year it was 151 days on the road, not counting races." He's a motivational speaker for corporate groups, talks to school kids, and does product endorsement, among other activities. That's in addition to raising sled dogs and watching his wife, Melanie, compete in stage races. In between, novice mushers come to Lincoln to learn firsthand how to compete in the Iditarod. But there is life for Doug outside dogsledding; in his two weeks of free time in the summer, he grabs a fly rod and heads for the streams.

Since Doug began racing in 1989, he's noted many changes in the sport. "Improved equipment, tougher races, and the caliber of the dogs is higher than ever," he observes. Of course the mushers have gotten better, too, and Doug's one of those responsible for raising the bar. ◆

David Healow is a third-generation Montana farmer, but unlike most crops, his need no water and survive in the worst soil. What's more, his plants take up 1/100 acre and pay for themselves in five or six years. David harvests the wind. Farming is a Montana tradition, and he views wind power like any other crop—"You put money in the ground, then harvest it." Even his Web site, www.montana marginalenergy.com, suggests that he's not your typical farmer. "The margins," he explains, "are crummy ground, the land that no one else will farm," which, he adds, "is most of Montana."

It's a labor of love. His real source of income is managing pain, either in the hospital as an anesthesiologist or at his private practice for pain management in Billings. It was in the early 1970s after he got his degree in microbiology at the University of Montana that he became acutely aware of the oil crisis. But while he was a medical student in the Southwest, he was taken in by solar adobes, and then wind power. His interest developed into something more concrete, which is why you can see his plants sprinkled throughout Montana.

Anyone driving the stretch of I–90 through Livingston can't help but notice David's towers standing in stark contrast to the natural beauty of the Absaroka Mountains. He installs and maintains them throughout Montana, but the only ones he owns are those in Livingston. This seems to be the perfect place for his machines because Livingston has notorious winds that have been known to blow over a railroad car. But David says, "It's not the best. The ideal wind must be steady at 20 to 30 miles per hour year-round and from one direction. Here it comes in spurts, but it's still not a bad place to put them." Decked out in coveralls, David tends to three of his machines erected on the town's former airstrip.

WIND FARMER

DAVID HEALOW, BILLINGS

Today two are running; the other is waiting for a part and stands mute in what David refers to as perfect Montana weather—windy, cold, overcast, raw. "The worse the weather, the better the wind. It's ideal from December through March." The functioning machines hum and whoosh, a rather comforting sound out on the prairie. He opens the door to the shack that stands at the base of the nearest one and throws a switch. The braking system brings the spinning blades to an abrupt halt. He flips the switch again and the wind catches the blades, turning them slowly for half a minute or so, then revving them up to speed. Another switch automatically comes on with a bang, throwing him onto the grid again.

David's search for the perfect wind takes him across the state. At promising sites he flies a kite with a monitor and about 200 feet of line attached. If he gets the readings he likes, he installs a pipe tower that he leaves in place for about a year to record the area's winds. Sometimes the best spot is on private property like the ranch in Greycliff whose owner uses one of David's machines to power the entire spread, cutting his power bill in half. In Livingston the whole town benefits, with the city receiving a 3 percent royalty. He wants to put up more wind plants, but the city hasn't been able to issue approval, and some citizens balk for aesthetic reasons, even though the plant is several miles out of town. His electric is sold wholesale to the power grid, and the royalty that is paid to the city helps reduce the tax base and saves it money.

Mention NorthWestern Energy to David, then stand back. He has no love for the power company, calling it perfidious, contumacious, rebarbative—you can be pretty sure that's not good. His smile belies the serious undertone, when he says, "Dealing with NWE management is like dealing with the Communist Party. It's not that they're against wind power; in fact, they encourage it, but the process is political and arbitrary, and they've been noncompliant with federal law enabling wind development." Wind plants have tremendous economic potential for Montana, but David has been frustrated by bureaucracy and "corporate misbehavior. I've been required to insure them against damage even though there's little to nothing that could make them a liability." What really gripes him is that NWE sells its power artificially low, making it tough to compete. Pending contracts issued by the power company will allow him some profit, but he's not about to quit his day job. More promising is the grant he received from its department that deals with low-income needs and renewable energy.

It's a David-and-Goliath situation: At 240 feet to the hub, NWE's machines are much larger than his 80-footers, but they all hum along at 120 mph with matching tip speeds and rpm that generate the same amount of power. The difference is in the cost. David's are recycled. He buys them used, rebuilds them, and then installs them for a third of the price of a new machine. "For the average person to put up a wind plant, it would run around $35,000, but that's not practical. Can you imagine a town with a turbine in everyone's backyard or people climbing the tower for repairs?" he asks.

But there is a future in wind, David believes. California is going to throw away four thousand machines, and he's taking as many as he can to rebuild and install, erecting them as he finds suitable sites. He envisions creating a small-town economy around wind. Ideally he'd like to put wind plants near towns whose agriculture has failed. He explains that many of these towns have abandoned machine shops that can be put back into service rebuilding and maintaining the plants, providing better-paying jobs. Even better than generating power, he sees a future in using his machines to produce hydrogen to run equipment and power cars. How soon will that happen? David smiles wryly and says, "The answer's still up in the air." ✦

"Welcome to heaven, here's your harp; welcome to hell, here's your accordion," reads the caption to a *Far Side* cartoon. Laughing, Peggie Pahrman says that's exactly the kind of accordion bashing she'd like to change. Then again, while the rest of the baby boomers were swooning over Fabian or singing along to the *Mickey Mouse Club* theme song, Peggie's idol was Myron Floren, the always grinning accordionist on the Lawrence Welk show.

That's why today the hills of Philipsburg are alive with the sound of music for three days each year at the Rocky Mountain Accordion Celebration (www.accordions.com). Make no mistake, this is not your typical concertgoing mosh pit crowd, and you can leave your Bic lighter at home. Even the local cops who have been brought in for "crowd control" are bored stiff, according to Peggie: "It's three days of calm madness."

ACCORDIONIST

PEGGIE PAHRMAN, PHILIPSBURG

Peggie was always interested in the accordion and took lessons for a while when in fifth grade. "I used to look at the Montgomery Ward catalog and wonder how I could get an accordion." Unlike many kids who were dead set against music lessons, she really enjoyed hers; but as she got older, her lifestyle changed and she packed away her squeeze-box, not to pick it up again for another forty years. It wasn't quite like riding a bike—"I'm not a natural musician. I have to practice hard"—but she kept at it. She hooked up with a friend in Missoula, who also played, and along with a core group of about twelve others formed the Five Valley Accordion Association, who gather to play every couple weeks.

She and her percussionist husband often attended the big festivals like the one in Kimberly, British Columbia. After one such trip her husband suggested they needed a festival closer to home, in a small town, and Philipsburg fit the bill. In 1995, after a year of convincing, planning, and promoting, the Rocky Mountain Accordion Celebration was born. Each August they come—from California, Colorado, Arizona, Canada, even as far as Virginia—these accordian-totin' jammers.

The centerpiece of the event is the stage— the *platzl*—and tented plywood dance floor, which takes up the better part of this colorful Victorian downtown's main street. The music is nonstop, with each group allotted twenty minutes in the spotlight. Onstage is Sweet Squeezins, an all-girl group—it's Peggie's turn to solo, but to look at her, you'd never know she was "having a ball. People tell me to smile, but it's not that I'm not having fun— I'm just really concentrating. I don't like playing in front of an audience but don't mind so much at the festival because these people are really great."

Folks are here to dance, have fun, listen to music, and dance some more, but it tends to be a low-key crowd, so there's not much drinking, and things don't get rowdy. These music lovers come by the hundreds, and there are more each year. They stay in motels and campgrounds, and more than one has spent the night on Peggie's living room floor. And you're just as likely to find them *playing* anywhere—bars, street corners, the bank, and of course onstage. Dancers begin early morning and go until they almost drop: fox-trot, polka, waltz, two-step, some jazz and big band tunes—and, oh yeah, the chicken dance. Those in the know will tell you that dancing on asphalt wears out the feet and legs—and that would be totally unacceptable— thus the plywood-paved street. Accordions have always gotten a bad rap because so much of the music was oompah-pah, which quickly gets dull. Rule number one: The music on the *platzl* has to be danceable, so you won't be inundated with "Lady of Spain" or "Roll Out the Barrel"—at least not often.

There's no general admission fee, but don't try to get on the dance floor without a festival button. If you don't buy one, you could find yourself in the polka pokey, chained to a light pole by the polka police until you pay. Sounds harsh but it won't be on your permanent record—it's all in fun. Not everything is free: You'll pay for the pancake breakfast, steak supper, and special concert at the opera house, where you'll find the top players and probably Peggie emceeing it. Vendors set up along the street to hawk their new and used instruments. An accordion can run from a decent used one at $300 to a top-of-the-line model at $1,200 and up—not for the casual player.

Planning an annual festival, practicing her accordion, and running her own gift shop take up all of Peggie's time. "I'm a sporadic practicer—I play once or twice a day for maybe three weeks, then get busy and may not touch the keys again for another month, which is bad." She smiles and adds, "How can I grow?" A store down the street offers live music every Sunday afternoon, inspiring Peggie to do the same, but she'd go one better and play for customers herself. It's the best of all worlds: She'll be able to practice and entertain shoppers as well as the occasional aficionado.

You don't have to own an accordion to participate in the festival. In fact, Peggie says, "We're still looking for a good washtub bass player, and to bring in some younger faces, we're hoping to get Cajun and zydeco groups."

Cajun, zydeco, big band, the chicken dance—there's something for everyone. You can't play the accordion and not have a sense of humor. It's a good time with a good crowd, and to Peggie it's like a slice of heaven. Welcome to Philipsburg; here's your accordion. ✦

Thanks to Jack Lepley, visitors to one of Fort Benton's main attractions not only have a good time but also leave with a better idea about working life on the rolling prairies of Montana. Each year nearly twenty thousand guests passing through the metal-sided building that serves as the Montana Agricultural Center and Museum of the Northern Great Plains are treated to Jack's inventive displays. "I didn't want a bunch of stuff in glass cases," he says, referring to the museum's open concept. What Jack has created is one of the more engaging museums in Montana—he's taken the ho-hum subject, at least to most of us, of agriculture and made it informative, even entertaining.

Opened in 1989, this repository of agricultural antiquities, tucked away on a side street, is run by the River and Plains Society. What began as cochairmanship of the planning committee devel-

MUSEUM CURATOR

JACK LEPLEY, FORT BENTON

oped into a full-time job when Jack suddenly found himself working solo. And although his job involves a lot of paperwork, meetings, grant writing, and management, it's the exhibits he really enjoys doing most. He read up on the finer points of creating displays and "picked the brains" of a handful of men who had homesteaded the area, for much of his historical data. "They also helped me track down museum items."

The men worked hard at finding rare and obscure artifacts from prairie life, but Jack finally convinced them to bring the more common, everyday items. "I wanted things that visitors could identify with, for people to say 'I remember having to use that,'" he says. On one wall hangs a complete selection of manual can openers, while cast-iron wrenches adorn another, and some of us still cringe at the collection—and memory—of rug beaters. There's a re-created root cellar filled with canned goods and the cobwebs that made us hate going in to retrieve Mom's canned peaches.

With no formal training Jack has planned, researched, and built every display, first sketching out ideas on a yellow pad. This fourth-generation Montanan is well traveled and, whenever he can, checks out other museums for inspiration. And he needs lots because he also has a hand in the Museum of the Upper Missouri and several historical homes in Fort Benton. His background as a teacher and coach comes through in the details—visual and written.

Jack was raised as a town kid and never worked in agriculture, but you'd never know it from the Ag Center's displays of everyday life in an agricultural society. During economic downturns like the Depression and war, farmers resorted to other sources of income, including bootlegging and egg sales, and there are exhibits that document these activities as well as the problems with drought and machinery failure. Handmade aprons and quilts hang on a backyard clothesline, and a fully set table is waiting for farmhands to wash up and sit down to dinner. The history of irrigation spans several walls, and more than one visitor has paused to read how young boys herded hundreds of turkeys to control invasions of grasshoppers.

He throws out little if anything, salvaging machinery pieces, especially those bearing the manufacturer's name, to stand out as a work of art. And he's turned a collection of old metal tractor seats into a farming still life. Even the machinery—and there's plenty of it—is often shown in context. A rundown Model T sits derelict as it was left, complete with rust, tumbleweeds, and flat tires, against a barbwire fence. The five-millionth tractor produced by International Harvester nearly fills a room. All the Montana dealers chipped in to buy it, then used it as a promotion at their franchises. When the novelty wore off, they donated it. Jack feels it's a priceless, one-of-a-kind item.

Jack credits Montana State University with the idea of segmenting the region's agricultural history into three periods: pre-Depression, the

Depression era to World War II, and postwar. But once again his creativity kicked in, resulting in a series of three windows that look into the same room setting from three different periods. Each setting has identical items in the same place—a wall clock, telephone, coatrack with hat and coat, calendar, reading glasses, campaign pin, newspaper, and so on. Viewers can see how times changed by comparing items between rooms. It's the kind of clever idea that makes the museum so entertaining.

Like a proud father, Jack points out Montana's little-known claim to fame: the Hornaday bison. Sharing a setting surrounded by five other behemoths, this is not your everyday park animal but a special bison that was used as the model for the buffalo nickel.

All of the museum's artifacts are either an outright contribution or on permanent display. "I didn't want to create a setting for something and then have the donor ask for the item back," he says. The museum's not adding to its bulging archives—there's just not enough room—but Jack's careful to rotate exhibits to keep things fresh and people coming back. Along with the items often come the stories behind them, which Jack incorporates into his arrangements.

The main building is expansive, but so is the museum's collection; there's enough to fill a town, and it does. Out back on two acres is a reconstructed 1920s Main Street with a post office, law firm, general store, pharmacy (one of the finest collections anywhere), blacksmith shop, gas station, and more. Many of the buildings were originals, brought in to complete the cityscape. Like any thriving town, it's growing and changing—a depot and dress shop are in the works.

Travel brochures for Fort Benton tout it as the Birthplace of Montana and boast of its colorful reputation as one of the wildest towns in the Old West. Its famous transients Lewis and Clark are long gone; so are the gunslingers and frontiersmen, but agriculture is alive and well—it's living history. And Jack wants to make sure we don't forget. ◆

I've had an exciting life," says Marion Hanson. At the very least, it's been full. This Baker octogenarian has a lot to look back on. Most recently she was named Montana Mother of the Year; before that Lady Senior Citizen of the Year. She's a member of the Fallon County Council on Aging and the county historical society; active in the church; and part of the hospital helpers. She says she's young at heart and loves to dance and rarely misses an exercise class, three days a week, no less. At her peak she was cranking out forty quilt tops a year and still quilts every Wednesday with a group of church women. She helped author the book *O'Fallon Flashback* and has been writing local news for fifty-five years. Marion says she's satisfied with five hours of sleep a night. "I'm actually in bed for eight, but I'm thinking." Yet if you really want to know about one of the more unusual aspects of her life, just mention grasshoppers. She remembers . . .

GRASSHOPPER INVASION HISTORIAN

MARION HANSON, BAKER

It was 1938, and along with the rest of the country, the people of Baker were still recovering from the Great Depression but feeling optimistic. After suffering through years of drought and hail, the area was enjoying a wet spring—crops could be good this year; surely the worst was over. At the time, Marion was a young woman living on the family homestead, just outside of town, in Willard. Like so many others she mistook the dark cloud on the eastern horizon as smoke billowing from a fire in a nearby oil well. But this cloud made noise. As it got larger and closer, it droned like an oncoming airplane. "The cloud blocked out the sun," she says. "But this wasn't smoke—rather, millions and millions of ravenous grasshoppers." It was July 2, and Marion will never forget it.

No one knows for certain what brought the hungry hoppers to the area—it certainly was not an annual event. Locals speculated that because the weather that year had been unusually dry and hot, it was perfect for developing a bumper crop of hungry hoppers. They came from dry areas miles away, moving as far west as Terry and north and east into the Dakotas. They were migrating and, because they cannot or do not fly in cool air, had to land, and Baker became the landing strip.

This arrival was more than just a few annoying insects. In the mountains where cooler temperatures forced them down, they were piled 4 feet deep; the roads had to be cleared with snow-plows, and everywhere driving was dangerously slick. Their clouds were so large that planes couldn't avoid them.

It's one thing to imagine what the invasion and devastation were like, but Marion remembers the details. "When my father realized what was happening, he told us all to go inside. The hoppers hit the windows and we could hear them slam against the house—they sounded like hail." The grasshoppers stayed only a few days before moving on, but while they were here, life

became unbearable for the already stressed-out ranchers. If you did go outside you had to keep your mouth closed, and "We had to keep the milk pail covered when we went from the barn to the house. On top of that the cows moved around so much to avoid the hoppers that they were jittery and weren't giving much milk to begin with."

The grasshoppers ate everything, even the clothes off the washline, all except for heavy double-stitched seams. Marion says, "We had to stand at the clothesline with swatters to keep them away." The family car (theirs had a rumble seat and side curtains) wasn't spared either; the critters ate almost anything not metal. One woman riding to church in a rumble seat had holes eaten in her dress by the time she got there. Marion recalls, "They even ate the siding off the house, and we had to store the pitchforks with their handles in the hay or they'd eat them too."

But it was the crops that suffered most. Knowing what kind of damage the hoppers could do, farmers cut their rye early and late in the day, hoping to harvest it before the hoppers could get it. In spite of their efforts, many insects were bound into the bundles because they would cling to the stems to avoid the cool ground. Records show that one bundle of rye was found to have 1,850 grasshoppers in it, not counting loose pieces; in another field a bale of hay yielded a gallon of the voracious vermin.

Marion's homestead had two hundred chickens, who at first must have thought someone broke a piñata, but soon even they tired of them. "Because of the chickens we weren't as bad off as most—we had eggs to sell. We also had a root cellar, and Mom had canned meat, so we could ride out the invasion, but others lost everything in their gardens. We salvaged potatoes, and in fact Dad sold a carload to Idaho. It's how we paid our taxes that year."

After a few days, life got back to normal. The only thing left behind were piles and piles of dead, decaying hoppers and a stench that was impossible to ignore. Ever the lady, Marion says, "The air had a disagreeable odor, but even that wasn't the end of it." The next year saw a big hatch of baby hoppers from eggs left by their predecessors. Although they too dined on the vegetation, including garden plants, it wasn't quite like the initial invasion.

In the 1960s when Marion was postmaster, she recalls yet another grasshopper invasion, but it was nowhere near as bad as the dreadful summer of '38. In Baker those few dark days in July will always remain the benchmark by which all hopper invasions are measured. ◆

It's tough to find a Missoulian who's not hooked on the ponies, especially the kids, and one of the biggest kids at A Carousel for Missoula is Jerry Diettert. Although retired from cardiology, he still gets to work around bodies, only these are carousel horses. He waves his hand and emphasizes, "This is a community effort. I'm just one of the volunteer carvers and hundreds of people who brought this thing together." And no one is likely to argue with an expert wielding a sharp instrument.

A local cabinetmaker was inspired to construct a community carousel like one seen on a trip to Spokane. He offered to donate the horses if the city would put up the land. After the go-ahead he realized he'd need carvers and advertised a class for fifty people— one hundred showed up, including Jerry. But "I didn't make the cut," so he and his wife, Ethel, volunteered as sanders, which eventually led to carving.

CAROUSEL CARVER

JERRY DIETTERT, MISSOULA

It takes about one thousand hours to create one horse, which begins with a sketch on heavy paper that's transferred to the basswood traditionally used. Two-inch-thick planks are assembled with dowels and glued with "lots of clamps. Everything is hand-carved, hand-sanded, hand-painted," Jerry says. To keep the weight down, the inside is hollow, a perfect place to hold mementos such as photos, letters, or other memorabilia. Many are signed inside as well.

The carousel is more than horses on a platform. It's an expression of the community, but you can't express yourself without funds, so an organization was set up: "Our fundraising committee had it pretty easy. People were eager to participate and the project had great support and loads of publicity." Within six months all thirty-eight horses had been "adopted" by individuals, families, or businesses at $2,500 each. "If you adopted a horse you got to sit down with our artist to design it." This led to the most creative horses on any carousel. "We had a contest—the grade schools that raised the most pennies would get their own horse." The result is four horses known as Pennyponies, decorated with some of the coins.

Each horse is unique. Some have the sponsoring company's logo worked into the motif; one is adorned with tennis balls, symbolic of the adoptee's love for the sport; a construction company has a hand plane on the back of the saddle, a saw on the side. But the entire carousel is personalized: If you look carefully you can find Jerry's stethoscope in the carved artwork. The dragon holding the brass rings wears a wedding band because one woman told her carver husband that the dragon sees him more than she does, so he put a ring on it. When they were all finished, all of the workers carved their initials on the tall tree trunk where the dragon is perched.

"The other carvers used to joke that I wasn't allowed to have sharp instruments when I was in practice," Jerry laughs. The only carving he'd done before tackling horses was a half-baked mallard decoy, but to look at his horse—Pal's Pal— you'd never know it. Pal was the parrot who always rode on the shoulder of Sam Caras, Jerry's father-in-law. The horse is decorated with flowers and ribbons to represent the Caras flower shop, but most notable is Pal, who rides just behind the saddle. "He was the hardest part—I spent many hours looking at parrot photos before beginning."

On Memorial Day 1995, Missoula turned out for the parade that kicked off the carousel's opening. Nearly four years after the initial carving class, the first rider plunked down 50 cents for a four-minute ride back to childhood on the fastest carousel in the United States. Spinning at 8 miles per hour, riders are required to BUCKLE UP—IT'S THE LAW, according to signs posted above each horse.

Jerry suggested that they needed a volunteer organization to carry on after the carousel was finished, so they formed the Ponykeepers, who provide daily maintenance and run the rig, decked out in costume on holidays. Following a tradition of sorts, they carve horses for new carousels—and charities—who use the animals as fund-raisers. Pony rides alone don't keep oats in the feed bin, so the Ponykeepers sell carvings and do restoration. "People buy them for living room decor, and some that we've restored are more than one hundred years old," says Jerry.

Thousands of people zip past Missoula on the interstate. Wanting a highway sign to draw in passersby, the group approached the state but was turned down. Hoping to change the state's mind, they carved a Shoshone pony modeled after a pack-horse used by Lewis and Clark. Today the state has the horse but Missoula still doesn't have the sign.

Deciding to make a good thing even better, Jerry and a few others developed the idea for Dragon Hollow, a playground adjacent to the carousel. For nine days, four thousand volunteers sawed and hammered to build a playland created by kids themselves. "We surveyed the children and found that a castle scored big, so that became its centerpiece."

The carousel is open New Year's Eve, which ties in to one of Jerry's many volunteer pro-grams—First Night. "It's a way for people to cele-brate in a safe and nonalcoholic way at more than a dozen venues," he notes. When Jerry's not work-ing on the business end of a horse, he's focused on community, tutoring homeless students who are behind in their work. He's also writing a book about the Caras family, for whom the carousel park is named. When not serving as a Ponykeeper or dragon park guy, he's ushering gridiron fans at Griz games at his alma mater.

Jerry's no stranger to carousels; he rode the one at Columbia Gardens in Butte and took his own kids there years later. Today in Missoula he takes his grandchildren, but it's not just a ride; it's a family heritage—that just happens to go 8 miles an hour. ◆

Call the Larimer household and you'll get a recording with Whitney's voice that says the usual: "Hi. We can't take your call right now," yada yada yada. That's because Whitney's either skiing, playing basketball, at her church youth group, or at play practice. Or maybe she's planning her next soap box derby run. This Bozeman beauty is one of Montana's lesser-known celebrities, having gone to Akron to race in the All-American Soap Box Derby.

Whitney didn't even know what a soap box car was when her father saw an ad in the *Bozeman Chronicle* for "racers wanted." His enthusiasm wasn't exactly contagious, and Whitney calmly suggested, "Let's look into it a little more." The next thing you know, their noses were pressed against the window watching for the delivery truck with their $500 car kit.

Unlike NASCAR, a soap box derby is kids racing against kids in nonmotorized cars made

SOAP BOX DERBY RACER
WHITNEY LARIMER, BOZEMAN

by the kids themselves—with the big finale in Ohio. Compare this race with a Cat-Griz game for notoriety except the race is known internationally (not that the game isn't). More than four hundred kids show up from all sorts of foreign places, including Montana, to whiz down a hill at 28 miles an hour to "Fight Your Way to the Bottom."

The soap box derby, like the Monopoly game, was one of the few good things to come out of the Depression. It began in 1934 with actual soap boxes, empty crates, and old baby-buggy wheels and evolved over the years to sleek plastic shells transporting kids adorned with safety helmets down a 989-foot slope to the checkered flag.

Plane tickets to Akron don't automatically come with the car kit—you have to earn your place at the top of the hill. It all starts with the car, and there are strict rules for assembly because it undergoes thorough inspection before being allowed to race. Construction is supposed to be by the driver, not the parent, and because Whitney has always been a hands-on person, she had no trouble recognizing a hammer from pliers. With her father's supervision she did more than 95 percent of the work on number 110 Plum Loco, which she spray-painted in the backyard. To standardize each vehicle, weight is added inside, so Whitney learned how to use a torch to cut the railroad track steel, which she painted purple. With the tires' rubber so thin—ironic because the main event is in a town known as Rubber City—she didn't want to risk damaging them on a practice run, but "I got to sit in it on the sawhorses."

The big day in Bozeman came mid-June, but Whitney's debut didn't go exactly as planned. Her brakes failed, and as she got to the bottom of the track she deftly steered around the hay bales but plowed into a nearby pickup. She was unharmed but the soap box car wasn't. They stayed up all night making repairs—with lettering tape

they put a big Band-Aid on it—but she was out of the running for Akron.

As any sports fan knows, "There's always next year," but for Whitney it nearly wasn't: A freak June snow canceled the race, which was rescheduled for the following weekend. The delay didn't hurt a bit—this time she beat out twenty-five competitors. Her secret: "I have a gentle hand. I don't jerk the steering wheel but go straight ahead, and I hunker down to get as aerodynamic as I can." With her car crated and shipped off to Akron, she and her family were on their way—almost. On the runway in Bozeman they were told their flight was canceled, and they spent the next ten hours in the airport before being sent home. After several more glitches the following day, they finally arrived in Cleveland, but Whitney's bag went to Florida, so they went shopping to outfit her for the week's stay at racing camp.

The racers were treated like royalty, with police escort everywhere they went. The week kicked off with introductions, after which each racer was given a parade through town. "While they announced my name and read off my interests, I tossed Montana souvenirs to the crowd—we all did." The next two days were spent fine-tuning and qualifying the car, which is when Whitney learned that two of her washers were the wrong size and one of the weights had to be ⅛ inch shorter—and it had to be corrected in twenty minutes. Unlike some people who came equipped to repair the Hubble telescope, their tool kit was your basic wrench, screwdriver, and sandpaper, but they managed to find someone to cut the iron.

Half an hour before Whitney raced, it poured, and Dad did the only natural thing: covered the car to keep the bearings dry with the Montana flag that Whitney carried in the parade. The view from the top was intimidating; this was not Grant Street in Bozeman but Derby Downs, the official course built just for the event. Whitney was fearless. After her practice run she said, "Dad, I could hear the wind in my helmet, and it was great." Almost as great as her run—twenty-nine seconds later a photo finish determined that she came in second by half a wheel length.

Bozeman's derby has lost steam as well as financial backing, and its future is uncertain, but not Whitney's—even if she's not zooming down a racetrack, this girl is a go-getter. She's part of a percussion ensemble, a creative-thinking group, the jazz band, and the chorus in the school musical. In spring her thoughts turn to track and field. And winning isn't limited to racing: She got first place in the Invention Convention. After hearing stories about how her grandfather slowly labored over opening Christmas presents to save the paper, she invented a gizmo to open them quickly yet salvage the wrapping.

Although her future is not written in stone, she thinks being a "veterinarian or maybe an engineer would be neat." And she's not ruling out another shot at Akron. ✦

Ask folks about their fascination with railroads and you'll get a variety of answers. One that surfaces frequently is "It's the romance," not the hot-and-heavy-breathing kind but rather the excitement, the unknown, the adventure—lost in jet travel. But railroads are a large part of our country's history, especially in road-starved Montana, where so much has depended on trains.

Alberton resident Darrel Dewald might not consider himself a romantic but he does love the railroad. As a onetime brakeman, flagman, baggage handler, and conductor for the Milwaukee Road, he saw it as more than just a job. "It's a family thing," he says proudly. "My grandfather worked as an engineer, my father and uncles were conductors, and I have two sons who are engineers." Now retired, Darrel began this love affair in 1944 and for the most part enjoyed every minute of it.

Railroads can make or break a town, and Alberton was no exception. Its 350 residents were

---

RAILROADER

DARREL DEWALD, ALBERTON

---

there because of the Milwaukee Road, one of the country's most noted railroads, whose routes formed a spiderweb across the United States. Darrel says, "We thought of our Lines West stretch from Mobridge, South Dakota, to Tacoma as the main rail. We had separate work schedules and separate union committees; we didn't even consider Lines East as part of the same railroad." Like most railways, the Milwaukee Road tended to bypass larger towns, but sitting midway between Deer Lodge and Avery, Idaho, Alberton was more than just a whistle-stop, it was a terminal point where crews were changed.

Darrel's career began as a brakeman, handling switches and coupling air hoses, and he especially liked the Blackfoot line, hauling logs to Bonner. It was a great job, but metal parts and Montana winters weren't a good match: "We had to nudge the cars to loosen their frozen wheels; now it's not a problem—all are roller bearings."

Four years later he was a conductor. He made sure that the train operated correctly. Each car had a waybill, noting what was in it, where it was headed, and most important that it was on time. Darrel's biggest brush with history was in the late 1950s when he worked on the electric Little Joe engine. The Joes (Big Joe was nothing more than two Little Joes put together) were named for Soviet leader Joseph Stalin because they were made for Russia, but President Truman embargoed them, so they were put to use stateside.

For three years he also worked the passenger route on the Columbian and Hiawatha trains that ran from Deer Lodge to Spokane. His was the voice we associate with railroads, when he'd call out "All aboard," coaxing travelers out of the "beanery." He admits that as much as he liked interacting with people, he still preferred the freight trains.

"I was always serious about my job; any neglect could have caused so much damage." A runaway train might be fun at Disney World, but it's nothing Darrel wanted to deal with. To make sure the brakes were in shape, officials would "pull a signal test," a practice emergency stop. But Darrel remembers one that didn't go as planned: "We had such short notice and hit the brakes so hard that sparks flew and started the hills on fire." In spite of all the practice, getting a five thousand-ton train to stop quickly is wishful thinking—at 40 miles per hour it takes at least a mile. "One time there were kids on the rail and we had to 'dump the air' [make an emergency stop], not enough to make the train jump the tracks, but it sure gives the caboose a jolt as each car bumps up against the one in front. By the time the caboose gets there it's like hitting a wall."

Unfortunately, collisions are inevitable and many of the victims are animals, domestic and wild. Surprisingly the biggest animals weren't the biggest problem: "We hated hitting sheep. Their wool would get tangled in the electric motors' armatures and ignite—the smell was awful."

In 1980 the Milwaukee Road pulled out of Alberton, and Darrel watched it go: "It was a sad day." Forced to go to the Burlington Northern in Missoula, he says, "It's the only time I didn't like my job: lousy shifts and being at the bottom of the pecking order." Yet he hung around for another three years before retiring.

These days he's still surrounded by the railroad, including remnants of the big yard, turntable, and roundhouse that lie between Main Street and the interstate. When he's not trying to sort out the piles of railroad memorabilia in his basement, he visits the Milwaukee Railroad Museum, which he helped get started, appropriately housed in a pair of railroad cars.

Thousands of train enthusiasts collect, restore, and re-create the glory days of the railroad, whether with models and layouts at home or playing conductor-for-a-day on real bygone relics; however, Alberton's not likely to have such a renaissance. "They removed our tracks and the railroad bed is now a housing development," Darrel says, but that doesn't stop the people from coming. Each summer mobs descend on this small town to celebrate Railroad Days.

Part of the allure of rail travel is the hypnotic clickity-clack of the wheels, but even that's changed. The rhythmic sound was caused by the train going over the rail joints, but now they're ribbon rail, which is welded, and only an occasional clack can be heard. One thing that has held steady is the whistle, which is always blown at crossings— two longs, one short, one long.

There's something about a passing train that compels people to wave, and it's a rare engineer who doesn't give one in return. Although Darrel laughs loudly at the notion that blowing the whistle and waving are an engineer's only responsibilities, he finds himself giving each passing train a knowing nod and smiles when he gets a wave back. ✦

At Conrad High, students call him Mr. Gus, but in Montana's bars, he's known as Erik "Fingers" Ray. That's because when he's not teaching advanced math, he's on the road performing. Typical is one summer night in Belt, where you can hear "Brown-Eyed Girl" half a block down from the Brew Pub, the one with all the pickups and one Honda CRV parked out front. It's rodeo weekend, and the place is packed. You step inside expecting a full band—and there is—but there's only one musician on stage: Erik Gustafson.

Tonight, decked out in western gear, a cup of unidentified liquid refreshment nearby, this Montana lounge singer has the crowd rocking. At once Erik plays the drum, guitar, harmonica, and cymbals, all while singing—like patting your head while rubbing your stomach. "I can do that, too," he says. Nearly three hundred songs clutter his head, but he works from a list of about half that,

ONE-MAN BAND

ERIK GUSTAFSON, CONRAD

depending on the crowd. "Sometimes I forget a line but I can fake it and no one usually knows the difference." One routine is country, another rock and roll, plus a little jazz and blues, but he gladly takes requests.

They ask for everything from Broadway show tunes to Metallica—"I don't do them"—but the strangest request was for the theme from the TV show *Roseanne*. "I don't even know what that is." He was forced to learn "Country Roads" for a wedding, which he now performs reggae style. "It wasn't so bad—kind of like learning to eat asparagus," he laughs. "Brown-Eyed Girl" is most requested because "all the girls think I'm singing to them. I play it at least three times a night."

Erik enjoys when the crowd chimes in with "yippee-ki-ay"'s on "Ghost Riders in the Sky" but generally doesn't like people performing with him. "One fellow wouldn't stop playing his harmonica, so I grabbed the thing and stomped it until it flattened." To avoid confrontation he asks nicely three times, but "I won't tolerate anyone messing with my equipment." Asking politely doesn't always work, and Erik learned a valuable lesson: "Never hit a Norwegian in the forehead— go for the jaw instead," but notes that he finished one more song before going to the emergency room. Outdoor gigs like rodeos present a different, less violent, problem: "I did an outside thing in June on the Missouri River where the mosquitoes were so bad, you couldn't open your mouth to sing."

Sometimes opening his mouth *is* the problem: "I did a song about the Griz that I think may have jinxed them" (as soon as he put it on a CD, they lost). "It's sold a few copies perhaps because of its unkind remarks about the Bobcats," he jokes. Although he's never been fired from a job, he did a parody of a song about an unridable horse that nearly emptied a barroom in Whitehall. "It was a bit dirty and offended some folks, but one couple requested it for the first dance at their wedding." Erik shakes his head. "Their first dance as a married couple. Go figure." Off-color lyrics were never an issue at Luke's, a biker bar in Missoula where Erik made his name.

Perhaps it was prophetic that his music career began with a high school band called Mayhem. In the late 1970s he and his brother had a band in college, too, putting themselves through school with it. The group was called Time but later changed to the even less dynamic name of Talk. They played from Vancouver to Denver and have a couple albums to prove it, "but I keep them hidden." After experimenting with new wave music, he tired of it and moved back to the family ranch, where putting in fourteen-hour days wasn't any better, so he got a solo act at the Palomino Bar in East Glacier, five nights a week. "I still did ranch work in the daytime, though."

Erik heard about a one-man band in Idaho and liked the idea of not having to deal with musicians. He found that there are about a dozen such bands, especially in jazz and blues, but he's pretty sure he's the only one in Montana—at least one who teaches and ranches. "My music means I can afford to teach, which I love." He rarely plays at school but admits that once he twanged out the school song by vibrating a plastic ruler. At the end of the day, he heads home to his herd of forty cows (all named), which is as eclectic as his musical repertoire: "They aren't registered—they're the most colorful herd in the county."

Most jobs are within 100 miles of Conrad, but it's not unusual to find him in Bozeman, Plentywood, or Seattle. He racks up 35,000 miles a year, staying at the luxurious Chevy Motel. "That's anywhere I park," he quips, referring to the van he had welding students customize. "I know every good turnout in the state—my favorite is milepost 164 on Highway 2."

Erik started his career playing a Harmony guitar: Now he collects them. "You may have wanted a Fender or Gibson, but if you couldn't afford them, you got a Harmony. It was nearly every kid's first." He claims he doesn't have a favorite song or performer—it always changes—but he does like "the old blues guys," and he stays away from modern country: "It's not really country anymore." His teenage kids think his music is geeky, and "I think theirs is 'devil music.'"

Erik's been performing at places like the Brew Pub—and in the classroom—for several decades, enjoying both immensely, but he looks forward to retirement when "I can run my cows and do more gigs." As he finishes off a Hendrix classic, a sneaker-clad cowboy, beer in hand, shuffles through the peanut shells littering the sanded cement dance floor to grab his gal for her favorite song. Erik graciously breaks into "Brown-Eyed Girl" for the fourth time that night. ◆

Clad in shorts and polo shirt, Jim Janke dons his floppy hat and sunscreen to begin another day of retirement, but he's not heading off to the golf course. He and his wife, Marian, grab a couple of five-gallon buckets and drive off to dig in the dirt. Their home for the summer is Sapphire Village, set in some of the prettiest rolling hills ever surrounded by mountains, in central Montana. But this chunk of the Little Belts is known for more than scenery; it's home to one of the most sought-after gems in the world—the Yogo sapphire.

This town, with a handful of permanent residents, isn't even on the state map, but it has a watering hole where they gather to celebrate and commiserate over the day's findings. It's the only place in Montana for Yogos, which is why these treasure hunters have paid a premium for the privilege to dig here. And Jim, a CPA from Billings, is one of them: "I started with faceting, then heard

---

SAPPHIRE MINER

JIM JANKE, BILLINGS

---

about the Yogos, and we've been coming here since the late 1980s."

Even to an untrained eye, Yogos stand out: They're known for their distinctive color and purity. Most gemologists agree that other sapphires can't hold a candle to the Yogo. Jim says, "Other sapphires need to be heat-treated to bring out their color—Yogos don't. That's what makes them the most precious gems mined in the United States. Smaller stones fetch hundreds, and a one-carat rock can be worth several thousand dollars."

Jim's shiny black bus that he calls home stands in sharp contrast to the other seasonal residences. He says, "It has everything we need," an understatement, considering it could accommodate a touring rock group. Each morning he and Marian load digging gear into their road-weary pickup. A couple miles down the road they stop to unlock the gate to the main mine and their part of it—a 15-by-15-foot plot. Like many hobbies, you learn by doing, and Jim has become an amateur geologist of sorts, explaining that Montana's topography is perfect for gems, Yogo Gulch in particular. The deposit runs about 5 miles long and is 7,000 feet deep. The property was once owned by a British corporation, which mined the gems that adorn the queen's tiara. But there are all sorts of legends as to who actually discovered the Yogos: a sheepherder, gold miner Jake Hoover, and even Charlie Russell.

Jim says they are allowed to remove four buckets per plot per day, which doesn't sound like much unless you're the one doing the digging and lifting. "There's a lot of work involved. The whole process goes like this: dig, haul, screen, wash, sort, hunt with tweezers, and hope you don't lose the tiny stones you find." Deeper is better; some diggers go down 20 feet or more, requiring ladders for access, but cave-ins are a concern so many sites are braced, giving the area a look of an oversize ant farm. Jim says that if your plot is a dud, you can move your stakes to an unmarked area and start all over.

Once his buckets are filled with promising-looking concentrate (dirt, to the layperson), Jim hauls them back to the campsite for processing. Near the bright clean bus stands an assortment of old equipment that at first appears to be abandoned, but each has its function. A cement mixer removes loose dirt and washes the gravel, which then goes to a motorized jig that shakes the daylights out of it before being dumped into screens. Jim then puts them into a stock tank filled with water and swirls them to get any sapphires to sink to the bottom of the screens. When they're flipped over onto worktables, sapphires are now visible at the top of the pile. Then it comes down to good eyes and tweezers: Jim carefully picks out anything that looks interesting and puts it into a small bottle, which is where rule number one comes in: Keep the cap on the bottle no matter what size you find. "We learned that the hard way."

The largest Yogo is on display at the Smithsonian Institution, weighing in at just over 10 carats, but most average a third of that. Jim's largest find was 4.5 carats, which he cut in half. "It was too thin to do much else with—you lose two-thirds of the original stone when it's cut—so I made two stones out of it and sold them to a local orthodontist." Although it doesn't quite measure up to Princess Di's nine-carat engagement ring, the one Jim made for Marian has more significance behind it. "I thought that after fifty years of marriage she needed a nice ring," Jim says. Even though he sells some of his stones, not all are destined for jewelry, and he keeps an inventory on hand that "I bring out to look at just for fun."

Montana has a bunch of monikers: Big Sky State, Big Sky Country, Place Where Summer Might Fall on a Weekend, but its official nickname is the Treasure State. Yogo sapphires, along with the agate, are a main part of the reason why. "One legend suggests that Yogo is a Native American word for 'blue sky,' " according to Jim. Although sapphires come in every color except red, they rank right up there with diamonds, and the white stones are often used as a substitute. Their colors are gained from iron and titanium, and the stones are composed mostly of aluminum oxide, but few people care. All they know is the signature cornflower blue—a bit deeper blue than a Montana sky on a clear day.

At the end of the summer, Jim and Marian close the doors to the bus and point its nose southwest toward California's warmer climates. Clad in shorts and polo shirt, Jim dons his floppy hat and sunscreen and begins another day of retirement, but this time he's heading off to the golf course. ◆

Bill Bell's a man of few words, but he's definitely more talkative than his clients. He never wanted to be a mortician; his dad pressured him into it. After his first semester at mortuary science school, he wanted to switch to premed, but his mother knew it would upset his father and talked Bill into sticking with it. Maybe his aversion to the family business had something to do with the way he was introduced to it. "When I was in high school, Dad made me dig graves by hand for $8.00 a hole. Chipping away at the hard soil was slow going." He notes that the minimum depth was 5 feet, but "Dad wanted a half foot more. I split the money with my buddy who helped me. We liked going out at night, chasing girls, so we dug from midnight through to morning." But his youth wasn't wasted just on grave digging: "I learned embalming when I was in eighth grade, too," he adds.

He grew up in Malta, where both sides of his family homesteaded, and his parents became the biggest dryland farmers in Phillips County, "dryland," he says, "because there isn't enough water to irrigate." His father did about sixty-five funerals a year, and he ranched. When Bill finished mortician school in St. Louis following World War II, he came home to run the ranch and the funeral home, but when an opportunity opened up in Glasgow to run a funeral home there, he left. In lightly populated Valley County, there weren't enough people dying to sustain the two mortuaries, so Bill merged with his competitor and eventually bought him out.

Bill's one of the lucky people who could make a living by combining three diverse backgrounds—mortician, rancher, and pilot. Buying out his sister's share in the early 1970s, he took over the family ranch, built a 2,000-head feedlot on the 9,000-acre spread, and lost money on it. While in the service he got his first taste of flying, which he later put to good use as a crop duster; besides, "fly-

MORTICIAN

BILL BELL, GLASGOW

ing was the best way to get around the ranch." But what he enjoyed most was taking ambulance patients to Billings, Rochester, or Minneapolis. "I'm still amazed at how much it's changed: Back then it cost $250 to fly a patient to Billings, now it's $4,800." At one time he had as many as six planes, three of them solely for crop dusting. When he wasn't winging his way over the prairie, he managed the funeral home, but even pilots aren't immune to being grounded, and after several heart bypasses he gave up flying.

Glasgow fits the national annual average of 8.2 deaths per 1,000 people, so including the reservation population, Bill does about one hundred funerals a year. Mortuary science has become a family tradition, intentional or not. Two of his sons as well as a grandson have followed in the business: "I nudged one of them but the other went into it himself, as did my grandson." Unlike his father, Bill insisted that his boys have another degree, something to fall back on. Lately he has less involvement with the funerals, leaving that to his sons, and

focuses instead on carving and sandblasting headstones in a building on the west edge of town.

As you enter the shop, Bill nods toward a mezzanine that holds an antique first-call fire wagon from the Helena Fire Department—first-call because it holds three barrels and buckets and a quick hitch hookup for emergencies. "I always loved old things," says Bill. Indeed he does: A stop in his building is like a visit to a museum. The headstones take up a small part; the rest is devoured by other projects. He's known for his buggy collection that includes scattered pieces as well as finely restored antiques. Just about anything you can think of is somewhere in the building. Among the six or so buggies and wagons are irrigation pioneer H. H. Nelson's wife's personal buggy and the town's restored wagon hearse that he uses for funerals on request.

Valley Monument also houses a pump organ, huge motor home, unusual diesel-powered golf cart, 1957 Jaguar, 1915 Dodge, 1932 Ford pickup (the first V-8 Ford built), a small boat that was confiscated from drug runners, a motorcycle, and a stud cart (a small horse cart once used for traveling stud service). It's a good thing he put a back door on the building because there's a lot more outside, including one of his favorites, the cannon that's shot off at high school football games.

Bill's day is full. Every morning a group of men show up for coffee at BILL'S BEANERY, marked by a hand-carved sign that someone tacked up above his office door. While the guys down java, he gets to work on headstones. Images of a man hunched over a slab, chisel in hand, laboriously chipping away flakes of rock, give way to modern technology. Near the coffeemaker is a computer for designing and creating the templates used to sandblast the stone. The method of carving isn't the only thing to change in his business; the customer has a wider range of material and color choices, but don't think you'll save a bundle on providing your own rock—it accounts for only about a third of the price. When the coffee crowd is long gone, Bill spends his quiet time restoring old furniture, often until late at night.

Northern winters can make burial a challenge. In some states bodies are stored until spring thaw, although Bill doesn't think that happens in Montana. He does say cold weather is a factor, not necessarily a problem. "There's nothing colder than a cemetery, and the worst thing you can have is a priest with earmuffs." He laughs at the notion that morticians are a serious bunch and has plenty of stories to back that up. He especially appreciates the inscription on one woman's headstone that reads, WE HAD A GREAT TIME.

Amen to that. ✦

ABOUT THE AUTHORS

John and Durrae Johanek start out all their trips from Bozeman, Montana. When they're not exploring the four corners of the state, they have real jobs. To keep the family car's gas tank topped off, John is a magazine design consultant and partner in Ayers/Johanek Publication Design, Inc. He also writes a regular column for *Editors Only* and is a frequent contributor to *Folio* and other publishing trade magazines. Durrae keeps herself occupied by working eight days a week as an editorial freelancer. She lives with her two cats, two goats, and John, not necessarily in that order. She has a degree in English from Kutztown University in Pennsylvania and has written several nature-related magazine articles appearing in *Bird Watcher's Digest* and *Popular Mechanics*. Their appetite for Montana is as big as the state itself. They enjoy birding, wildlife watching, and cross-country skiing. Whenever they can, they take to the back roads in search of all three, and even a gumbo road or two.

ABOUT THE PHOTOGRAPHER

Kurt Keller is a commercial and fine-art photographer living in Helena, Montana. He was formally trained and earned degrees in photography at Rochester Institute of Technology and Kent State University. He enjoys lazy summer afternoons with a fly rod in hand and spending time with his wife and two sons. He has been photographing the people, places, and spirit of Montana since 1993.